How To Be
Happy If You
MARRY
AGAIN

All about Children, Money, Sex, Lawyers,
Ex-Husbands, Ex-Wives, and Past Memories

Carmel Berman Reingold

PERENNIAL LIBRARY
Harper & Row, Publishers
New York, Hagerstown,
San Francisco, London

For Harry,

without whom there would have been no remarriage
for me to enjoy . . . and no *Remarriage* to write

This book was originally published in hardcover by Harper & Row
under the title *Remarriage.*

HOW TO BE HAPPY IF YOU MARRY AGAIN. Copyright © 1976 by
Carmel Berman Reingold. All rights reserved. Printed in the United
States of America. No part of this book may be used or reproduced in
any manner whatsoever without written permission except in the case
of brief quotations embodied in critical articles and reviews. For information address Harper & Row, Publishers, Inc., 10 East 53d Street,
New York, N.Y. 10022. Published simultaneously in Canada by Fitz-
henry & Whiteside Limited, Toronto.

Designed by Eve Kirch Callahan

First PERENNIAL LIBRARY edition published 1977

STANDARD BOOK NUMBER: 06–080412–2

77 78 79 80 81 5 4 3 2 1

Contents

Acknowledgments

A Very Special Appreciation to . . . Norman J. Levy, M.D. who, as a psychiatrist and a friend, spent a great deal of time discussing with me the various nuances of remarriage. His help and insights permeate much of this book.

AND MY THANKS TO . . . the many people I interviewed. They were candid, direct, and most willing to give of their time, and of themselves, to this project. They allowed me to tape their thoughts and emotions regarding all aspects of remarriage, and I'm grateful to all. I would enter their names here, if it were not for my promise to them of anonymity.

I

The Facts Are ...

The divorce rate has nearly doubled since 1960.
There were an estimated 970,000 divorces in 1974.
One out of three marriages ends in divorce.

But ...

Four out of five divorced men will marry again.
Three out of four divorced women will marry again.
One out of every four marriages is a second, third, or
fourth marriage by a widowed or divorced person.

And ...

Seventy-five percent of all divorced people remarry within
five years.
It is estimated that close to a million children are affected
by the remarriages that take place each year.
Two out of five remarriages will end in divorce.

But Don't Worry About the Facts

People are remarrying all the time. The rate of first
marriages has gone down, that's true, but the rate of
remarriages has gone up. There were nearly 2.2 million
marriages performed in 1974, and this was 2.4 percent
fewer than the marriages performed in 1973, but a hefty

30 percent of that 2.2 million were people who were getting married again.

Is it because they didn't learn anything the first time, and they're being foolhardy? No, say psychiatrists, psychologists, and lawyers. It is because they learned a lot the first time and they're willing to try again, equipped with a lot more understanding and knowledge of how to make a marriage work. Four out of five divorced people remarry within five years, and depending on the study that you read, either two out of five or three out of five of these remarriages end in divorce.

Why do the statistics differ? And why is the divorce rate among people who remarry so high? Statistics are compiled by a series of projections rather than by a minute analysis, and they should be regarded as generally true, but not as gospel. The divorce rate among people who remarry seems high because there are some people who continue to marry and divorce, marry and divorce ad infinitum. This is their way of life, but because statistics concern themselves with numbers rather than people, one small segment can cause an imbalance when the figures are applied to the entire group.

This book is not about statistics; it is about people. It's about people who have remarried, and realized that a remarriage brings with it a new love, and a new set of problems.

"The first time I got married," said one man, "I was worried about love, sex, compatibility, making a living, and what my friends and family would think of my wife. The second time around, I had all that to think about plus my children and my stepchildren, hassles with the lawyer, and hassles with my ex. I wasn't worried about making a living anymore, but I was worried about alimony and child support."

That, painted with a broad brush, outlines some of the

facets of remarriage. But there are nuances of emotion, levels of coping, and a tremendous variety in possible life styles to consider.

Investigating remarriage means asking about divorce, widowhood, children, family, and an extensive network of relationships. My information came from interviewing people around the country who are remarried, and from the people who have peripheral dealings with them, as lawyers and analysts do.

My happiest discovery was the positive, good feeling that most people had about remarriage—theirs, or others'. As I said, the statistics on divorce may be scary, but they apply mainly to one segment of people who remarry, rather than to the entire group.

Dr. Norman J. Levy, a psychiatrist practicing in New York, who was kind enough to make himself available for extensive interviews, and who is a Fellow of the American Academy of Psychoanalysis and a professor at the Postgraduate Center for Mental Health, has confirmed this by reiterating that remarriages can be happy and successful, if people have learned from the mistakes of the past.

"If people have grown through their personal experiences, tragedies, and pain, this can give them a certain new dimension, as well as appreciation and understanding."

Is this true for all people who remarry? No, and here's where that statistic on the high divorce rate among the remarried comes in. Dr. Levy says there are people who are "narcissistic . . . people who want to be told they're charming, they're witty, they're clever, they're lovely, and they can have anything they want, all the time. These are the people who are more likely to marry, divorce, marry, divorce, and so on. But if the man or woman has learned something from the first experience, if the first divorce is not just something that ended in bitterness and acrimony, and without learning, then the subsequent choice in a remarriage would be more in keeping with what they learned about themselves. In a good remarriage, people act to fulfill their healthier—rather than sicker—needs."

Most of the people I interviewed were forward-looking, outgoing and open. They were aware of the problems presented in a remarriage, and they expressed their feelings freely. I was overwhelmed by the openness of the people I spoke to, most of whom were candid about their thoughts and emotions, and spoke without subterfuge. They talked, they complained, sometimes they called days later to relate an additional point they had forgotten to make, but through all they said ran twin threads of commitment and caring. These people were dedicated—not just to remarriage, but to being happy when remarried.

Can a person who is remarried or planning to remarry learn from these experiences? This isn't a "how to" book with all the answers, but it can be a "how to" book in another sense.

Lao-tse said that "Man does not have to go out into the world to learn of the world of men"; man, the Chinese philosopher implied, has only to examine his own heart and mind.

In somewhat the same way, reading about the experiences, both good and bad, of people involved in circumstances similar to your own, and examining them, can be fruitful. First, it tells you that you're not alone—you're not the only wicked stepmother around, or you're not the only man who deeply resents writing that alimony check. *You are not alone.* That's always good to know. And good to know, too, is the fact that other people have found working solutions to problems like yours. It is understandable that their solutions may not be yours, but as you identify with their experiences, you may find it easier to come up with your own answers.

Many people I interviewed said that they had to work at their remarriages; work is fine, but it's drudgery if it's not combined with love and optimism, and it was both love and optimism that I found in great abundance among people who are remarried.

Raoul Lionel Felder, one of the top matrimonial lawyers in this country, confirms this: "I've observed over a number of years that some people think that the people who are getting divorced are disillusioned people. Quite the contrary. The divorced people are the most hopeful. If you believe in marriage, then you also believe that if you've got a lousy marriage, there's a good one over the horizon. So you get divorced, and go on to—hopefully—a happy marriage. It's the cynics, who feel that this is not the best of all possible worlds, and everything's crummy anyway, who stay trapped in a bad marriage."

Forget the statistics, then. They're fine to know if you're trying to win a bet, but much more to the point for your life are the experiences of people like you who, facing the future with love and hope, have remarried.

II

Memories Can Kill ...
and Memories Can Save

"My second marriage was actually destroyed by memories of my first marriage. I kept remembering my first husband, who had died of a heart attack, and comparing my second husband to him. My second husband came off second best. I had no right to be surprised when he asked me for a divorce after just one year."

Stephanie L., Minnesota

"He was always calling me by his ex-wife's name. Finally, I told him that if he was thinking of her so much, maybe he'd better go back to her."

Paula J., New York

"Compared to that terrible guy she was married to, I've got to come off like a saint."

Barney B., Texas

Memories can kill a remarriage—and this means both good memories and bad ones. There's the widow whose second husband just can't live up to her remembrance of her first, and there's the man involved in his second marriage who's always afraid that his current wife will be just as impossible as his first.

"Sometimes," said Helena B., a thirty-year-old executive secretary from Michigan, "I want to tell Josh that I really feel he should do more things around the house. After all, I'm a working woman as well as a wife, and I'm pretty tired when I get home from the office, but I can't help remembering Josh's complaints about his ex-wife. It seems she always wanted everything to be on a quid pro quo basis. You know the kind of thing: I'll do the bookkeeping for your office, but you have to do the dishes and take care of the kids every night this week.

"That's why I'm afraid to ask Josh to help. I'm afraid that I'll remind him of his ex-wife."

Helena is afraid to remind Josh of his unhappy first marriage, while Bill feels that his wife is constantly comparing him unfavorably to her first husband, who died of a heart attack in his late thirties.

"I can't believe that Marge's husband was that perfect," said Bill W., "but the way she remembers it, he must have been some kind of a saint."

"Joe wasn't a saint," said Marge, who was married to Bill for one year, after having been widowed for six. "I know he wasn't perfect, but he was a quiet, gentle guy. Bill is lively, outgoing, and has a terrific sense of humor, but he shouts like crazy when he gets mad. I can't help it. I keep thinking that Joe never shouted, never yelled, never talked to me that way."

What to do about memories? They can't be jettisoned like so much excess baggage—not unless you acquire a convenient case of amnesia with each new marriage.

One highly successful advertising woman had the answer that worked for her. When asked if she could be interviewed for this book, she said, "Look, this is my third marriage, and I've never been happier. It's true I've canceled three appointments to be interviewed, but you've got to understand, I don't want to rake up the past, I don't even want to think about it. If possible, I'd like to pretend that it never happened."

"You Know the Definition of a Bachelor?"

One couple, both widowed before they married each other, who work together running a restaurant in an exclusive California resort, have their own way of coping with their pasts—and the memories they engender.

"My first marriage was not a big success," said the husband, "even though we did stick it out together, but I don't try to eliminate the past from my mind. I can't. What I try to do is to remember the mistakes, and not make them again.

"You know the definition of a bachelor? A bachelor is a man who doesn't make the same mistake once. Anyway, I look upon my second marriage as my second chance—a way that I can redeem the mistakes of my first marriage.

"Listen, you've got to recognize your mistakes. You've got to have the courage to try and figure out why the first marriage was a failure, a flop, a nonsuccess. And then you correct those mistakes. You face things in a second marriage the way you never did in your first. The first time—you know—everything is all painted a certain way. Life is a bowl of cherries, rosy, things like that. After a while you realize that's all a falsehood, and by the second time, you get down to reality, and the memories can help you do that. That's the way I look at it."

His wife, Amanda, who serves so graciously as hostess in their restaurant that she gives all the guests the feeling that they're dining in her own home, has another way of dealing with remembrances. Her first marriage was happy and her second is happy, and her second husband is a great deal like her first. Both men were extremely successful restaurateurs and innkeepers, and both were extremely hard-working and oriented toward money and success.

"My First Husband and My Second Are Very Much Alike"

"I try to brush remembrances from my mind," said Amanda. "Every once in a while they do occur but I try to brush them immediately from my mind. I think it helped that I didn't remarry until six years after Justin died.

"And now that I am remarried, it's like my first marriage in a lot of ways. I'm still involved in business with my husband, just the way I was the first time. Of course, the second time things are a lot easier. I mean, in our age group [both are in their fifties] the children are grown and married, and there are no money problems.

"But I'll tell you, I think that memories are a very different thing for two people who have lost their first spouses. It's very different from people who are divorced. I don't know if I could marry a divorced man.

"It's not that I think divorced people are bad risks, or anything like that, but I don't think I'd care to live in the same world, knowing that my husband's former wife was still circulating. That's because I'm basically a jealous woman—but I'm not jealous of the past."

"I Was Like a Good German Hausfrau"

Regina and Olan P. have been married for ten years. It's a second marriage for both, and Regina admits that memories of her first marriage cause her to short-change Olan in some ways.

"When I was married the first time, I cooked, and

cleaned, and did the marketing, and ran the house perfectly. I was such a good German hausfrau—just the way my mother had been in the old country. Now it's different. When I married Olan I decided that I was going to be loved in spite of the fact that I was sloppy. It's sad in a way, because now I'm married to a man who really deserves to be catered to the way I catered to my first husband. Because Olan does cater to me, while my first husband did nothing but try to denigrate me.

"But I remember what he did, and I don't do enough for Olan, I know that. There's a stubborn streak in me because I was so badly burned by one man. Because of that, I've been the most stubborn bitch; and I see myself, I know how I'm acting, but I can't see myself wiping the floor for another man. And Olan deserves it, because he would do it for me, but somehow I'm no longer interested in proving myself as a woman through that channel."

Where is the Regina of yesteryear, or yesterday's marriage, who kept house so beautifully, and even helped put her first husband through law school? She's disappeared into the Regina of today, who takes separate vacations, who's involved in her job as a computer programmer, and who says she feels that all the men who played an important role in her life are envious of her.

"I don't know what it is, but I seem to arouse a certain envy, either because of my achievements—which don't seem to me such a big deal, but which may seem so to my husbands—or because of my personality. Anyway, I remember my first husband saying at the apex of the breakup of our marriage, 'You're not the star anymore,' and I never knew I was; I never thought of myself that way.

"But I can see that now with Olan—he seems to think that I have a spotlight on me."

The past does come back to haunt. As one charter boat captain said, "When you get married again, your new wife has got to be prepared for hassles—especially hassles out of the past."

Many people enter a remarriage thinking that they know what they have to face:

Children
Ex-wives and ex-husbands
Money problems
Loss of friends
Interfering relatives

They know about all those things, and they believe that they're equipped to cope. What come as a surprise are the shadows, the ephemerals.

"I'm Not Taking Anything Away From Him"

"When I got married to a widow," said Pete M., a construction engineer in New Mexico, "I felt I had nothing to be jealous about. My wife's husband had been dead for many years—how could I be jealous of a dead man? I even said, 'I'm not taking anything away from him.' But now I feel as though he's still around, because my wife says, 'Phil did things this way, Phil did things that way. . . .' And she makes him sound so perfect. Like he was some kind of saint. Look, nobody is that good. It's just that since he died, she remembers only the good things about him, and none of the bad."

Death does seem to sanctify the past, and to clean up memories. Why remember bad things about people who aren't around to explain or defend themselves? Remembrances are often kinder than realities. There is the myth that the widow or widower who was truly happy in a marriage will remarry quickly; but that is a myth. Divorced people remarry more quickly, because comparisons and happy memories of the past do not stand in their way. To the contrary, after a divorce, the new looks a lot better than the old.

But even a divorced person who remarries can use remembrances to hurt a new spouse.

A midwestern schoolteacher complained about the very detailed way her new husband related anecdotes.

"I know that Ed and his wife spent every summer of their married life at Lake Geneva in Wisconsin, and very often, when we were with other people, Ed would talk about the fishing up there. But he wouldn't just talk about the *fishing;* he'd always go into great detail about, 'May and I rented this four-room cottage right on the edge of the lake, and May's sister and brother-in-law spent one weekend each summer with us. . . .' May, May, May, and that damn cottage!"

"What's There to Talk About?"

How much censoring of memories does a husband or wife involved in a remarriage have the right to expect?

"Quite a lot," was the answer given by a woman in Chicago who was married for the second time to a man who had also been married before. "I watch what I'm saying all the time, so why can't he? I had a great time with my first husband. We traveled all over Europe, and we had a fantastic life together. My first husband died in his early thirties, but if I go to a restaurant or a hotel in Paris with my second husband that I had been to with my first, I don't bring it up. I wish my husband wouldn't bring up his ex-wife all the time. After all, he had a rotten marriage, so what's there to talk about?"

What's there to talk about? According to this woman's husband, everything. He has total recall, and he cannot relate any anecdote without filling his listener in on every detail. If he wants to talk about something that happened to him on an airplane flight, he must also mention that he was escorting his daughter back East to school, even though that has nothing to do with the point of his story.

"I'm so tired of hearing about his ex, and his kids, and his ex's family," his second wife complained, "I feel he thinks more about them than he does about me."

A Michigan doctor had a different point of view: "I don't mind hearing my wife talk about her ex-husband. Bring it out in the open, I say. I'd rather have that than wonder if she is thinking about him."

Memories are tricky things, and can be used as weapons. It's all very well for the seemingly innocent to say, "I'm entitled to my remembrances of the past," but that entitlement can be achieved silently.

As Dr. Norman J. Levy, the psychiatrist, put it, "You've got a mouth, but you've also got a head"—and that head should tell you when it's kinder to leave certain things unsaid.

"I Wouldn't Even Trust My Friends"

One happily remarried Pittsburgh woman said, "I make a conscious effort not to speak of my late husband to my second. Sometimes I can't avoid it, and certainly in my own head I do remember, and sometimes even compare, but I keep those comparisons to myself, and I never discuss Husband Number One versus Husband Number Two with my friends. I wouldn't even trust my best friend with that kind of ammunition.

"I know my present husband is happy with the way I handle the situation. Maybe he isn't even aware that I am handling it, because he once said, 'I always forget that you were married before.'"

Comparisons can be invidious, but where two divorced people marry, much of their conversation is often devoted to their former spouses.

"He did this to me. . . ."

"She did that to me. . . ."

As time passes, and they build up new experiences, some of the past is erased, but often, during very significant moments, one person may use the name of a former spouse, "Sometimes when I'm feeling warm and loving I will call my husband by my ex-husband's name, but usually when I do that, it's when I'm furious," admitted one woman.

James Thurber, author and humorist, who had been through some rocky marital times, expressed his feelings in a cartoon where a man is introducing one wife, while another crouches atop a bookcase. "That's my first wife up there," says the man, "and this is the present Mrs. Harris."

Memories seem less troublesome when each partner has been widowed, and where each has grown children. There seems to be a more dispassionate recognition of each person's right to the past.

Joan D., a highly successful attorney, was a widow with three children when she remarried.

"My two oldest were out on their own, and my youngest, Robert, was just ready to go to college, but then, he always came home for vacations and holidays, and the house took on an entirely different air for my second husband, into whose flat I moved. My husband was a widower with two children, and they were grown, too.

"Now, what is a greater reminder of your past marriage than your children? I mean, this one looks like his father—that's in my case. And maybe that one looks like his mother—as in my husband's case. Also, I'm on very close terms with my deceased husband's family, who continue to be part of my life, and my husband has to adjust to that. But on the whole, I think that remarrying when you're a widow is a lot easier than remarrying when you're divorced.

"Because if you're a widow, there are some occasions when you have feelings of guilt, but I don't think you're really saddled with it if you've had a good marriage. Whereas in a divorce you could always be thinking: Maybe if I had done this differently it would have worked out, or maybe if I had done that . . .

"Also, I think it's harder on the kids when there's a divorce and a remarriage. I think it's more difficult to supplant the parent when the other one is still living."

Memories do not kill a remarriage when they're placed in the proper perspective of the past. They are killers when they're used as bludgeons to make one partner feel that *You're not as good as she was,* or *You're just like he was, and I hated him. . . .*

"Compared to Those Memories . . ."

Virginia H., a biochemist, who married for the first time at twenty-nine, feels that her husband's memories of his ex-wife work only in her favor.

"I know the things that I'm good at," she says, "and I know the things that I'm bad at as a human being, and I'm so sure of so many things that I feel I'm a pretty terrific person for Andy. I can only be fantastic, in comparison to Joyce, his ex.

"That's part of the joys of a remarriage, as far as I can see. I mean, Andy's first wife was a woman who didn't work, didn't know how to balance a checkbook. She was not only a bitch, but a lazy person, incapable of making decisions, of doing anything independently of him, and so when I came along and started doing these things, he said, 'My God, you're fabulous,' and these were things I had been expected to do when I was practically five years old.

"My father gave me a lump sum of money when I went away to college and said, 'This is it. If you spend it in the first week, I don't want to hear about it. If you have all of it left at the end of the semester, it's yours. End of the story.' So I learned to manage money, and I was always a worker.

"Don't misunderstand me. I think that Andy is capable of doing everything better than most people, and I suppose his first wife, who was so helpless, fostered in him certain feelings of masculinity—you know, that 'I can take care of you, sweetie' syndrome. But I think it got out of hand, and I think he remembers that part of it, and he doesn't glamorize Joyce's helplessness.

"And then I came along, and said, 'Sweetie, this is not what I need, this is not how I need to be taken care of. You don't have to earn lots of money for me, or balance my checkbook. I need emotional taking care of, and sensitivity, and communicating.'

"Right after he moved in with me we had a big discussion. He said he didn't think he was ready for a relationship, or that he couldn't meet the demands I was making on him in terms of communicating, and normal things that one should be doing, and he said, 'You'll have to understand that I haven't done this for the eleven years that I was married to Joyce.' So I said, "You're not being fair to yourself. You think that I would have hooked my little hooks into you so fast if you weren't capable of doing all those things?'

"Andy's memories were bad—they were never glorified—and as I say, compared to those memories, I'm a pretty terrific person."

How Memories Can Save

Remembering why you married the first time or the last time—*the real why*—can go far toward making a remarriage work.

There are people who marry and divorce, marry and divorce, marry and divorce in a pattern of serial monogamy. And with each marriage, acquaintances may say, "Isn't his second wife just like his first?" Or "Doesn't her new husband remind you of her ex?" It's these people who swell the statistics on high divorce rates among people who remarry. What the statistics don't take into account is the fact that it is usually the *same* people who do all that remarrying.

As the philosopher Santayana said, "Those who do not remember the past are condemned to relive it." Similarly, if we don't learn from our mistakes, we are doomed to repeat them. However, happy remarriages are made by people who learn to examine themselves, their motives, and their needs.

As Dr. Levy says, "If the person learns, and doesn't see himself as the single aggrieved party, as the victim—and the other person as the sole aggressor and destructive one—then the second choice, or the next choice, would be more in keeping with what the person has learned about himself. Sometimes people have to go through a certain amount of therapy to recognize what went wrong, to see how they contributed to a marriage's failure. They have to ask themselves what made them choose a particular spouse, and what led them to get involved in a neurotic pattern. A remarriage can be a good marriage if a person has grown through his personal experience. Of course, narcissistic people will marry over and over again. There are men who just want to have a beautiful woman on their arm—someone to exhibit—and there are women who marry to be worshipped . . . to be adored . . . to be kept on a pedestal . . . to be fed the choicest morsels. And that's fine, but when they don't get those choice bits, they go on to the next man."

People who see marriage as a trade, a deal, an arrangement, marry frequently. *You give me this, and I'll give you that . . . and we'll stay married.* Happily ever after? Well, as long as the deal holds. But if you renege on your part of the bargain, don't expect me to fulfill my part.

Many people who remarry, and happily, have delved beneath their own public surfaces. They have questioned their motives and examined their fantasies. What did I want, that last time, when I walked down the aisle to the tune of that awful wedding march? What was I thinking of when I said "I do"?

Very often marriages end badly because they were based on everything but love. Social pressures may have played a large part: My mother wants me to get married, all my friends are getting married, if I don't get married this time, I may never get another chance. Or there are the rebellions against self, or against background: I am weak, therefore I want someone who is strong; I am timid, so I insist on someone who will be bold enough for both of us. Here is a person my family will never accept, therefore this is the perfect person for me; what a great weapon against encroaching Mama, bitter Father!

And then there are the climbing marriages—as pretty and fragrant as a honeysuckle vine on the surface, and just as deadly and parasitic to the lilac bush beneath. Marriage can be a step up in class, a step up toward money, an upward move toward social position. But all that mobility is flimsy if feeling is lacking. The honeysuckle vine is easily snipped if there's nothing to sustain it.

Remembering the real reason behind the marriage that *didn't* work can go far in preventing a similar mistake. Why did I marry someone who was so wrong for me? Something pushed me, but I won't be pushed like that again.

"Your first marriage," said a public relations executive, "is for your family and for your friends. Your second marriage is for yourself—because you're older, stronger, and surer about what you want out of life."

Remembering can help you avoid a mistake in choice; and it can also help you avoid the mistakes that made a marriage go sour. Since everyone's mistakes are unique, and highly varied, so are the solutions.

"I'm a lot more honest in my second marriage," said one man. "I no longer think that if we have an argument, our marriage will dissolve."

"I'm a lot less honest in my second marriage," said a woman. "I do my best to protect my husband, and to give him confidence. I don't point out each of his mistakes to him, the way I did with my first husband."

"I was Mrs. Adorable in my first marriage," said another wife. "I worked, and took care of the house, and never demanded a thing from my husband. Now things are different. My second husband and I share the chores."

Different answers for different people; different solutions, too. There are no insurance policies that guarantee a happy ending, but for many, self-knowledge and remembering can help.

Why Did I Get Married That First Time?

MELODY B.: Times have changed so much. I believe that I got married because I felt society's pressures. I met someone in college—that's about twenty years ago. He was very handsome—that was the one thing going for him. Everybody said, "Oh, he's so good-looking." And everybody else was getting married—there was a lot of pressure to get married. The pressure at that time was not to live with someone and not to be promiscuous, and I knew before I got married, and after I had been engaged and had all my bridal showers and all those things you used to do, that it was all a mistake.

But I went ahead. When I think about it now! It was such a big thing. My mother . . . and the dress had been bought . . . and I remember sitting there and saying to myself, I don't love him. But I went ahead, and I stayed married for fifteen years.

My present husband is so different from my ex. So different that I almost know how to anticipate Jay's—my present husband's—reaction, by knowing how my ex-husband would have reacted. My present husband's reaction will be absolutely opposite. Jay is absolutely right for me in every way.

Maybe second marriages are better because you get married for different reasons, and also, if you've had a bad first marriage, you just value your second marriage so much. Jay doesn't do dishes, and Jay doesn't take out garbage, and I could object, because I work very hard, but I don't, because I feel so warm and so happy. You make allowances with your second marriage. I don't nag. I very often realize that I could be saying, "Why don't you do this? And why don't you do that?" But I don't, because I don't want to jeopardize things.

CORRY D.: My first wife and I grew up in the same neighborhood. I was nineteen when I got married, and we had a child right off the bat—nine months into the marriage—and that meant many more responsibilities. Alice and I were married twelve years, but we only had one happy year. But we stayed together, and had three children. Twelve years and three children. The first one was a girl, and three years later another girl, and the boy came about during a reconciliation weekend which didn't work anyway, because things were on the rocks and there was really nothing that could be done. I guess I got married so young the first time because it's all the way you've been brought up, and you've been brainwashed. It's the "marriage is a bowl of cherries" baloney . . . marriage is happy . . . marriage is what you do. It's only after that you find out what marriage is really about: a lot of responsibility.

I don't think that many people who stay married in this country are happy. All, or most, of the married people I know—ninety percent—the people I see, the ones I grew up with, are not happy.

But my first marriage taught me something. It taught me not to take my second wife for granted. I try and help out with things now, even the cooking, though I wasn't brought up to do that. So what if you burn the food? Life is not so typecast anymore. My wife doesn't always do the marketing, though she does always do the ironing— I can't do that. But I know now that you can't keep a wife down on the farm barefoot—you know what I mean. You can call it liberating a woman, but it's also getting the man off his high horse.

ADELA B.: I was terribly impressed with my first husband and his family. He was this kind of an intellectual, reserved, deep; he was studying to be a lawyer when I met him. I helped put him through law school. And his family, they thought they were the cream, and I thought so, too. I was educated by my father-in-law, who was a brilliant man, but a miserable human being. They were unique people. But my husband intimidated me; he never thought I was as smart as he was. Now I'm not married to a man who's deeply intellectual. He's good, and he's understanding, and understands me. He's deeply emotional, and has a lot of insight. I miss the intellectual companionship, and I sometimes try to seek it elsewhere, but basically, in a marriage, this is very fulfilling—very physically fulfilling, also. And marriage is a compromise, isn't it?

SANFORD R.: I saw a bumper sticker on a car the other day, and it said, "Stamp out first marriages," and I think I'm for that. Well, the woman I married the first time, I thought she was the exact opposite of my mother, and I think now that was one of the main things. My mother was very religious—Jewish—and Grace, my first wife, was a Wasp from a halfway fancy suburb. It seemed fancy to me, because I come from an inner-city ghetto. Anyway, she seemed different, and that's what I wanted —someone different. And I thought she was a free and open person. I met her on Fire Island, and one night we were walking on the beach and I said how great if we could go swimming, and she just took her clothes off and dived right into the water. That's what I mean about free —not shy or shocked like the girls I knew in Brooklyn. And she was a terrific swimmer—also not like the girls in Brooklyn.

Anyway, this "different" girl turned out to be exactly like my mother—I mean, in a deeper sense. She was rigid, and cold, and critical, and nonsupportive. Everything I had been trying to get away from. She was always putting me down; she'd sneer at me for liking television, but she couldn't understand my taste in symphonic music. She was a great cook, only she wouldn't cook for me, and if I asked her to entertain some of my business friends, she'd do it—but she'd remind me that she had gone out of her way for me for weeks afterward.

Listen, I knew four months after we had gotten married that it was terrible, but I thought that's the way it was supposed to be. It hadn't been much better in my parents' house. I just didn't know, so I settled.

When I got married the second time, I didn't settle, but I didn't remarry until after two years of analysis. My second wife isn't anything like my first wife, and she isn't anything like my mother, either.

ELLEN W.: My mother and father were really responsible for my first marriage, because I got married to escape from them. They had applied tremendous pressure on me from the time I was a youngster, right out of college. They applied pressure because I wasn't married. They'd say, "You're the prettiest girl on the block, you're this, you're that, why don't you just stop futzing around and get married?" Their whole attitude was, they didn't understand why I had to go to college and why I wanted to go to graduate school—that almost slayed them—so marriage, my first marriage, was absolute escapism. It was the wrong person, the wrong time, the wrong situation, the wrong everything for me. I just wanted to get far away from them, and their nagging, and their control over me. I was very immature. I'd scream hysterically at them, but I'd eventually end up doing what they wanted me to do.

DEIRDRE R.: Everybody should be married once to prepare themselves for marriage. You really do learn from your mistakes. I was just too young the first time—seventeen—and I thought that it was the absolute end, the thing to do, to get married. When I got married the second time, I was more aware of myself—more aware of my second husband—more in touch with what I really wanted out of life.

HANK F.: I was very young, and I had known this girl in college, and she was terribly bright, and she went off to Europe on a Fulbright. When she came back, I just thought she was so bright, so smart—someone I could talk to forever. Thinking was a lot more important to me than feeling. She didn't know what she wanted to do, and by the time she got back I had a good job on Wall Street, and I think that impressed her, and I was glad I could impress somebody. Anyway, we got married, and over the next six years we had three kids—well, all our friends were having kids—and then one day my wife just said, "I don't want to be a mother, I don't want to be a wife, I want to play my guitar and go to art classes." Anyway, we were both unhappy, but my wife started going for therapy, and after a few times she came home and said, "There's no way that this is going to work at all. You have to go with me, because I'm getting so far ahead of you that we're going to lose track of each other." So I went to the therapist with her, and after a while, the therapist said, "Hank, we're spending all our time talking about how to cope with Fran's problems, and you're very patient, but someday your patience will run out." And that's what happened; my patience did run out. I stayed for a long time because of the kids, but I was unhappy for a long time, too. Fran didn't want me to leave—she really needs someone to take care of her—but being a caretaker just isn't the same as being a husband, is it?

Now I'm married again, to a girl who's just as smart as my ex-wife, but she doesn't make such a big deal about it. She feels things, and she talks about how she feels. She doesn't try to hide her feelings by intellectualizing them.

The other day she said, "You love me, don't you? Why don't you tell me so more often? I like to hear it."

I tried to explain that I don't talk that way, and she said, "That's a lot of shit." (That's how she talks; my ex-wife would have said *"merde."*) "You like it when I tell you how much I love you. Well, I feel the same way."

She's making me a lot less uptight. I've still got a way to go, but for the first time in my life I'm enjoying the warmth. I keep thinking about that book—you know, the one about the spy—and I think to myself I'm the guy who came in out of the cold.

CONNIE V.: I made the decision to marry when I was fifteen or sixteen, and I married my childhood sweetheart—the boy next door. It was almost incestuous—I had known him all my life—but then, I had a very sheltered life. I was not exposed to much experience; I really didn't know what the world was all about.

My husband was a high school teacher, and he convinced me that I was a dummy. He always used to say that I was sweet, that I was nice, but that I wasn't too smart. And I accepted that. You know how some men say, "You're not the most beautiful girl in the world, but I love you anyway." That was my first husband.

My life was very uncomplicated, but I always tried to search out interesting people, to make dinner parties, to create a little excitement. You have to understand my lack of exposure. My father was a truckdriver, my mother was a good *rugolach* baker, none of my friends went on to college, and I was involved with this boy— my first husband—and he was going to be a teacher. It was kind of a big deal.

I began to see that something was wrong with my marriage when my second child was accepted in an experimental nursery school program, and at that time I met this woman who was a professor—a super-bright lady—who said to me, "You're unbelievably smart. If

you had gone to college, you could have been president."
So I decided to go back to school and take courses that
nobody thought I could ever pass when I got out of high
school. I took German, and I got an A, even though I
had been bad in languages. That was the beginning of the
end. I felt like *The Education of H*Y*M*A*N*K*A*P*-
L*A*N*. It's almost embarrassing to look back and say
that at thirty I discovered Simone de Beauvoir.

Anyway, my first husband had an affair with one of
my close friends and decided he wanted to marry her,
but look, if the marriage had been spectacular and right,
he never would have played around. If I had wanted him
to stay, he would have stayed. I must have wanted him
and encouraged him to do what he did, so that he would
go and I'd be free. Because, finally, I was grown up. It's
harder when you're sixteen to make that kind of decision. You don't really know who you are, and you
haven't explored, and my first husband was four years
older than I was, and I thought he knew everything. But
you know, if I met him today I wouldn't even be his
friend—I mean, even if I had never known him before
—and that's because I was fifteen when I decided to
marry him, and now I'm grown up, and I'm not the same
person that I was then.

I waited ten years before I got married again, and my
second husband is a doctor and the director of community medicine at one of the hospitals in the city. And he's
so kind. Everyone loves him. You know how most people
are prejudiced against doctors? Well, everybody loves
Sam. Sometimes his patients bring him bags of vegeta-
bles if they don't have money.

You see, the second time around, I cleared it up in my
head as to what I needed and what was right for me—
and I also knew what I didn't need. I didn't need someone to help me raise the kids, and I didn't need someone
to help support them. I could do all that.

What I needed was a playmate, I needed a friend, and I needed someone I could really enjoy and have fun with, and share a very cerebral relationship with once my children were gone, because I knew at that point that they grow so quickly . . . and I wanted somebody who if we decided to retire at forty-five, we wouldn't dislike each other.

MARCIA F.: I got married the first time because I wanted to get away from my mother, who was an alcoholic. My father had deserted us when I was about ten, but whenever I thought about that time, it wasn't so much my father I missed as what he represented. We had lived in a nice suburb, and I had a pony, and we had lived in a big house—anyway, I remember it as being a big house. My father was a broker in New York, and he just took off with a much younger woman and divorced my mother, and I never saw him again. After that my mother started drinking, and I started eating, so that at eighteen I was terribly overweight.

Anyway, I met this dentist. He was a lot older than me, but he wanted to marry me, and it seemed like the only way out. I still think of him; he was awfully kind, and he taught me a lot. He was European, and being married to him was an education, but I think we both knew that I wasn't going to stay married to him forever. I got a job in a brokerage house (shades of my father) and worked my way up until I was one of the few women customer representatives at that time.

My second husband worked for the same company, and in a way he was a younger version of my father. Successful, good-looking, and highly erratic; married, too. I married him—and I can see now that in a way it was getting even with my father. I was going to do to another woman what my father had done to my mother and me. I simply had to marry that man; I had to get it out of my system. There was no way that marriage could have worked, because he really was like my father. My memories of my childhood came back to me while I was married to him. I remember my father shouting, my father striking out, my father drinking—and those were all the things my second husband did, too.

I am married again, and I really consider myself a third-time winner. My third husband has all the good characteristics of both my father and my first two husbands, but none of their bad ones. He's extremely successful, and that's very important to me—okay, I'm still the little kid who wants her pony, I admit it—but he's also kind, and warm, and very protective. He also admires me, admires my success, and doesn't compete with me, the way my second husband did—after all, we worked for the same company. It took me a long time to work things out. I know some people snicker a little when they hear I'm married for the third time, but so what? I had to get the past out of my system, and this marriage I know is for good.

FRANK V.: The first time I got married, it was just before I joined the Navy. Let's face it, I didn't know anything about sex—about women—and that wasn't the picture I had of myself. I was never too easy, too cool, with girls, so I figured the only way I'd make it was to get married. We stayed together the whole time I was in the service. She was really all right, and I was away a lot. But when I did my hitch, and I decided to go back to school on the G.I. Bill, I think we both saw that we didn't have that much in common. It was nobody's fault, but we got married for the wrong reasons. We both got married— you know the way it was then—just to get married. In those days it was some kind of a status thing for kids to be married.

I had plenty of status—I had the status of being a father, because my wife had twins. She went home to live with her parents and she had custody of the kids, and I went back to school. I took a course in business administration and went to work for a big food manufacturing company—you know the one. I met a girl at the company, and she was a bookkeeper. Not just a bookkeeper, but head bookkeeper. Well, we got married after a while, and she kept after me to get custody of the kids. My first wife still hadn't remarried, and my second kept saying, "What kind of a life is that for the kids? At least with us they would have two parents."

Listen, I'm sure my first wife was a perfectly fit mother, but my second wife really had me going, and I thought she was kind of sweet, wanting my kids and all. So I got a lawyer, and we did win custody of my kids. It was a bitter thing, and my first wife turned her back on all of us—our kids and me. Later I realized that my second wife, while she was good to the kids, had done all that because she just didn't want me to have any further contact with my ex-wife, and once the kids were with us there was no need for me to see her or send her child-support payments.

My second wife—it took me a while to see this—was a very manipulative person, and I know now that I'm an easy guy to do that to. After we got married, my second wife stopped working and stayed home with the kids. They were about eighteen when I met the woman I'm married to now. Believe me, she's a lot different from either of my earlier wives. We have a lot more in common than I had with my first wife, and she doesn't try to move me around like a pawn on a chessboard, the way my second wife did.

It was a funny thing, but after I told my kids that I was planning to divorce their stepmother, they went about looking up their own mother—she lives in another state. It was about ten years since they had seen her, and I learned that she had remarried and had a child.

You should have seen my daughter's wedding; she got married at eighteen. I have a feeling she didn't know which way to turn. Her stepmother and I were getting a divorce, I was getting married again, and it was a little too late to move in with her own mother. Anyway, everybody showed up at the wedding—my first ex-wife, my second ex-wife, and the woman who was about to be my third wife. She's been my third wife now for three years. You think I care what people say about being married three times? Hell, I've passed that barrier.

As a sage said, "Marriage is for the wise and constant, for when a divorced man marries a divorced woman, there are four minds in bed."

III

"They're My Children!"
"Yes, but They're My Stepchildren!"

"My husband's children from his first marriage have no manners at all. They never say 'thank you' or 'please'—not to me anyway. They treat me as though I were my husband's hired housekeeper and not his wife."

Lila P., South Dakota

"If I hear my wife's daughter say, 'But my *father* says,' one more time, I'm going to walk out."

Donald J., Ohio

"The first time my brother and I heard our stepmother introduce herself using *our* last name, we wanted to kill her. Only our mother is entitled to that name, and in the seven years that my father has been married to his second wife I've managed to avoid using our second name whenever I've introduced her to any of my friends."

Ginny F., New Jersey

According to the current crop of statistics, one out of three marriages in the United States ends in divorce. Last year of the approximately 970,000 divorces in the

United States, around 60 percent involved children under eighteen. Meanwhile, as the divorce rate climbs, so does that of remarriage. Close to a million children were affected by the approximately half-million remarriages in 1974. One in nine children today in America is a stepchild. Some 66 percent of divorced women, and 75 percent of divorced men, remarry within five years, and as they move into new relationships, their children enter the confusing, exciting, and sometimes difficult world of stepparents, stepbrothers and stepsisters, half-brothers and half-sisters, new homes or two homes, a life divided between one parent and another, time spent in a familiar environment and time spent in a new environment. Most parents agree that while divorce is a shock to their children, remarriage can be even more upsetting.

"I Cried, She Cried, the Kids Cried"

"I still remember the day I finally moved out and left my first wife," a man from New York said. "I cried, she cried, and our kids cried. Through it all, I got the feeling that my kids weren't really too surprised. They had heard us fighting plenty of times. But two years later, when I told my kids that I was getting married again, my son kept saying, 'I can't believe it, I just can't believe it.' My second wife and I have been married for more than two years, and my son still acts as though he can't believe it."

Many people who embark on a second marriage say "I do" to more than one person. There are his children. Or her children. Or both his and her children. And they are very real children. Not the 1.8 or 2.3 statistical average of children per marriage, but real flesh-and-blood kids who invariably regard a stepparent as an interloper.

"My Friends Told Me I Must Give"

Those who have children, but who have never coped with stepchildren, advise unremitting patience, tolerance, understanding, and love. As one young stepmother said:

"If I had listened to my friends, even my close ones, who told me that I must give, give, give and love, love, love no matter how my stepson behaved, I would have felt guilty, and wicked. Because I couldn't give and love without being loved, or at least liked, in return. My husband's son and I get along a lot better now that I don't let him push me around."

Television and movie melodramas perpetuate the myth that all a stepparent has to do is offer constant love, untiring patience, boundless understanding, and the children will come around. But even if some angel in human form could fulfill such unrealistic demands, most children would not respond with the love given to a natural parent.

"I Was the Only Father He Knew"

Glen L., from upstate New York, married his first wife after she came home from the hospital with an infant son. The baby's father had deserted soon after he learned his wife was pregnant.

"Andrea and I were married when her divorce came through," he said, "and I was the only father Jimmy ever knew. We told him that I was his stepfather, but I loved Jim, and I never treated him any differently than the three kids Andrea and I had together."

When the boy was sixteen his mother died of cancer, and Jim ran away to an aunt's house in another city. His

aunt—his mother's sister—insisted that Jim go home.
She, too, felt that the boy was really loved by his stepfather. Jim returned home, and stayed there until he was
eighteen. Then, no longer needing his stepfather's con-
sent, the boy joined the Marines and volunteered for
duty in Vietnam, where he was killed a few months later.

"What did I do wrong?" his stepfather has asked over
and over again. "I loved Jim, really loved him. He was
my son. Andrea and I wanted to send him to college, and
I know he wouldn't have joined up if she had lived. What
did I do wrong?"

Stepparents, as most of them sadly discover, don't
have to *do* anything to be wrong. They exist; that's
wrong enough for most children.

"I'm Just the Person Who Makes the Beds"

Pauline F., a New York widow who had no children of
her own, had looked forward to spending time with her
second husband's son and daughter.

"I had all those pictures in my mind of how it would
be," she said, "all those idyllic visions. I was going to
take Jenny to tea at the Plaza, and I could see myself
flying kites in the park with Joey, and visiting the zoo
with him."

Three years later, she has to admit that those idyllic
visions were also hopelessly naïve.

"As far as my husband's kids are concerned, I'm just
the person who makes the beds, cooks dinner, serves it,
and then washes up afterward. After all this time, if Joey
wants a glass of milk while we're having dinner, he'll ask
his father for it, expecting him to relay the request to me
—just as though I were a servant. And Jenny sees me
only as the competition—another woman, with whom
she vies for her father's attention. She's eleven now, but

when she was nine she was already saying, 'I went for a walk with Daddy, and I really gave him my sexy walk.' "

Because Jenny and Joey spend alternate weekends with him, their father feels that he can't be the disciplinarian that he might be if the children were living with him all the time. And like many men in the same situation, his own feelings of guilt dictate many of his actions.

"I Couldn't Stand the Antagonism"

"I love my second wife," a man in Boston said, "but I always have the terrible feeling that I have to choose between her and my children from my first marriage. That's the main reason I don't want any more children. I couldn't stand the antagonism between two sets of children."

Occasionally, a new baby does bring a family together. A widower with three boys who married for the second time said that his children didn't behave with warmth toward his second wife until they had a little girl.

"You should hear them! It's 'my sister this' and 'my sister that.' We're really a family now."

That's not the usual reaction, however. A schoolteacher in Baltimore said that her teen-age daughter reacted fairly well when she married for the second time.

"But when my husband and I had a baby, she insisted that she wanted to go live with her father and his second wife. That's where she is now, but I don't know where she'll go or what she'll do if they decide to have children."

Stepchildren can break up a remarriage, and many of them deliberately try to. The aggravation level with them is high, and stepparents have to be strong and very much in love to cope with the constant friction they create.

"My Second Husband Has No Children"

A magazine editor told a familiar story. "My husband
had four children from his first marriage, and with alimony and child-support payments, I knew I'd have to go
on working. I didn't mind that, but what I did mind was
having to wait on his children during their weekend
visits without ever hearing a word of thanks or appreciation.

"I suppose that real mothers don't get thanked very
often either, but they know they're loved. I knew I
wasn't. One Thanksgiving, things just got impossible.
I cooked a big meal. I set the table. I served dinner. I
cleared the table. Nobody made a move to help me the
whole time. Finally, I burst into tears. Those kids hadn't
talked to me through the whole meal. My husband felt
guilty and he insisted that the kids help me wash up.
Later on, one of them said, 'We don't really hate you,
Pat; it just looks that way.' That did it. My first husband
and I are divorced, and my second husband has no children."

"Food, Food, Beautiful Food"

A Dallas woman said, "I know that my husband's kids
think I'm the original wicked stepmother. I'll tell you, I
could rewrite that Cinderella story from the stepmother's point of view and change the whole image. But
I'm not going to let those kids break our marriage apart.
I just grit my teeth, take a Miltown, and cope."

One way of coping is to handle minor collisions with
humor. Take food, for example. It's axiomatic, most
stepparents agree, that children won't like their stepmother's cooking. She can be a great cook, but that has
nothing to do with their reactions.

One frequent comment, whether it's hamburgers or apple pie, is:

"It's not like Mommy makes."

A woman in Youngstown, Ohio, said that no matter what she prepared, her stepson would say, "Every bite tastes bad."

A Los Angeles housewife said that she plied her husband's son with steak, week after week, only to be told, "I hate steak." Finally, she switched to tuna fish sandwiches, and her husband received an indignant call from his ex-wife at his office.

"You're too cheap to feed our son decently," she said. "Stevie loves steak. And if I can buy steak on the little child-support money you give me, I don't think you have to feed him tuna fish!"

So Stevie's stepmother tried steak again. And sure enough, Stevie gobbled up every mouthful. When his stepmother expressed surprise, he looked up at her with large, injured eyes, and said, "But I love steak."

She had sense enough not to ask him how come he didn't like steak the first six times, because she knew he'd probably hate it again the very next week.

A young bride from Philadelphia reported on the dinner-table conversations when she first became a stepmother:

Week 1: "I don't like green salad. I only eat carrot sticks and sliced cucumbers."

Week 2: "I hate carrots, and the cucumbers aren't sliced thin enough."

Week 3: "I won't eat that brand of peanut butter."

Week 4: "I like that brand of peanut butter okay, but I hate grape jelly."

Week 5: "I also hate raspberry, strawberry, and currant jelly."

By the sixth week she arrived at a solution that has worked for her.

"I make the meals I'd prepare if the children weren't there—nothing too exotic or spicy, of course. If the kids are hungry enough, they eat. I've learned something that my stepchildren instinctively knew: Food isn't just food —it's a weapon. The first time my husband saw his children push their food away without eating it, I could see the guilt well up in him. I assured him that the children wouldn't starve, and that one meal missed wasn't a tragedy. I then made sure to serve him an extra-dry martini with a twist of lemon before the next meal.

"Now that I've stopped worrying about it, I've discovered that my stepchildren will eat almost everything. Of course, they've never complimented me on anything I've cooked, but I am taking empty plates back to the kitchen."

Wise stepparents also realize that it's not just the child they have to cope with, but ex-wives and ex-husbands as well. According to divorce lawyers, such as Robert Viet Sherwin, there is no such thing as a friendly divorce.

"If a couple is amicable," says Sherwin, "they stay married."

"If Your Mother Hadn't Left Me . . ."

Sonia R., happily married for the second time and living in San Francisco, says that she dreads the Sundays when her ex-husband comes to pick up their two boys.

"He always makes nasty comments about Bill, my second husband. He tells the kids their stepfather is sloppy. That Bill will never be a success, or make the money he does. Then he buys them expensive presents, and says, 'See, this is what you'd have all the time if your mother hadn't left me.' The children are hard to handle after that. I'm just grateful that Bill is blessed with so much patience. But once, when they kept needling him for a week about how he's not a big moneymaker, Bill lost his temper and said, 'If you think your father is so great, go live with him. But before you go, think about what you're giving up, like your mother, your school, and your friends. If you think it's still a better deal, let me know now and I'll help you pack. Otherwise, shut up.'

"They did, but I felt pretty terrible. I have to admit, though, that they're more respectful to Bill now."

"I Let Susan Wear My Sweater"

If a man has divorced his wife to marry someone else, his ex-wife is bound to react with anger and bitterness to anything and everything his second wife does, even though it may be to the advantage of her own children.

"Last time Susan spent the weekend with us," Marilyn J., from Boston, said, "it was pretty cold out. Susan had a coat, but no sweater. We were driving to the country, so I let Susan wear my cardigan. It was a little big, but we rolled up the sleeves and as Susan was wearing it beneath her coat, it was fine. I let Susan wear it home on Sunday night, and she returned it to me two weeks later.

" 'Mommy washed the sweater for you,' Susan said, innocently.

"I was tempted to say that the sweater hadn't been dirty, but I thanked her and let it go at that.

"A week later, I went to put on my sweater. Susan's mommy had washed it, all right. She had thrown my cashmere sweater into a washing machine with plenty of hot water and good strong detergent. Now the sweater is even too small for Susan."

Marilyn J. learned that she wasn't dealing only with Susan's mommy, but with her husband's ex-wife. She now knows it's best not to lend, or give, any of her clothing to a stepdaughter who's homeward bound. That innocent sweater triggered all kinds of resentment.

"Doesn't *she* think I know how to dress my own child?" Marilyn's husband heard the next day. "Besides, you never bought me a cashmere sweater."

Pauline F. bought her stepdaughter a hair bow because the child had admired one that she had been wearing. A few weeks later, the child asked, "Where'd you buy that white velvet bow with the streamers? Mommy said she'd get me another one."

"Why? What happened to the one I bought you?"

"Mommy dropped it accidentally in the kitchen sink."

A small matter, but a message from one woman to another that said, "I'm still here, and don't you forget it."

"You're Leaving Me"

Children—all children—know how to pull out all the stops. It's amazing how perfectly healthy, hearty children can suddenly look like large-eyed waifs from a Walter Keane painting. One Saturday night Lillian B., newly married and newly a stepmother, was going out to dinner with her husband and some friends.

She knew that her stepchildren were well used to the babysitter, but she and her husband decided not to leave until nine—after the kids' bedtime. Supper had been a moderate success, and the children had been played with, frolicked with, and amused the whole day.

And as Lillian said, "Remember, their day begins very, very early in the A.M."

The friends they were dining with arrived, as did the

babysitter. The kids were put into pajamas and all seemed well.

"Good night, Petey. Good night, Sally."

Kiss, kiss, Hug, hug.

"Wait! Wait!" A cry from Petey, who came pattering down the hall, a curly-headed angel in his Peanuts nightshirt.

"You're leaving me," he said to his father.

"Just for dinner, Petey. You know we're only going out for dinner."

"But that means I won't see you for twenty-four hours!"

The father said, "Just till tomorrow morning, Petey. That's only twelve hours—maybe even less."

"Then I must give you twelve hugs," said Petey.

And then and there a scene took place that would have made Charles Dickens weep. The father got down on his knees, while Petey proceeded to give him twelve clinging hugs, as the guests, the baby-sitter, the stepmother, and the big sister all looked on.

Later that night at dinner, the father was not only misty-eyed, but psychologically affected. Even though he had been divorced for three years, he called his second wife by his first wife's name a number of times. There was an embarrassing scene unforgivable in better restaurants. They're still together as of this, but as Lillian says, "We can't go back to that restaurant again."

"I did learn one thing from that evening," Lillian said. "It's a small matter, but with stepchildren every little thing counts. We try not to go out on the evenings the children are with us. Instead, we have people in. It means cooking and serving two dinners, one for the kids and another for us, but it's better."

Most of the problems stepchildren cause are not dramatic, earth-shaking events. An adult can usually deal with a direct confrontation. But children's tactics can be insidious, and will have the same effect as water drip-drip-dripping on a rock. One either works out a rapprochement with stepchildren or watches a marriage erode.

The couples who are still together are the ones who've acted with firmness. They have not allowed guilt, or the fear of losing a child's love, dictate their actions.

"When I stopped expecting Jenny or Joey to love me," Pauline F. said, "and accepted the fact that the best we could ever be to each other is friends—and that only when they're adults—the pressure was off. Our relationship is mostly calm now, occasionally pleasant, and always slightly cool. You might call it a truce, but it's far better than the painful battles we used to have."

"Better Earlier Than Late"

Unfortunately, children equal guilt to many divorced parents, and also to parents not yet divorced. Many couples stay unhappily together, while one or both operates on a secret timetable:

I will get a divorce when my kids are graduated from high school. . . .

I will get a divorce when my kids start college. . . .

I will get a divorce when my kids get married. . . .

Planning for a divorce years in advance means that the intervening years aren't happy ones, and according to many psychologists and psychiatrists, the parents are not really doing the children any favors by continuing a relationship in which the warmth has evaporated. The illusion of "togetherness," of "family," is maintained, but it is just an illusion, not sustained by any real coming together of husband and wife. Children are not really deceived by this kind of make-believe, and if they eventually come to blame themselves for a divorce, they are equally unrealistic in blaming themselves for the withdrawal or animosity that they witness between their parents.

Dr. Frank Curran, a child psychiatrist, was asked in a television interview if there was any special age that made divorce easier for the child. "My personal feeling," replied Dr. Curran, "is that when the parents can no longer get along, and they have sought professional help, and they feel that the marriage should break up, it ought to break up—and better earlier than late. I don't think the parents should wait for the child to be sixteen.

"I think it should be done when the parents decide. This is not only for the best interests of the parents, but also for the best interest of the child. The parents may stay together, but there's so much tension and anxiety that the children pick it up. The children are in a constant state of turmoil, and there's a constant division of feelings. If the parents are definitely committed to a divorce, then the sooner it is done, the better."

Yes, but that's not what my mother thinks, or my father says. And then my Uncle Joe said if I got a divorce now, it would be terrible for the kids. And that's what my business partner said, too, not to mention my next-door neighbor.

God, said a cynical general, is on the side of the big guns. Without being cynical, but recognizing the need that everyone occasionally has for big guns when faced with the opinions of family and friends—well-meaning, possibly, but just as possibly mistaken—here are some big guns to quote:

DR. J. LOUISE DESPERT, associate professor of psychology at Cornell, child psychiatrist, and author of *Children of Divorce:* "It is not always so traumatic for the younger child when his parents divorce. First of all, younger children have their own clarity inside. It's harder for older children, but they deal with it in their own way."

DR. NORMAN J. LEVY, psychiatrist, psychoanalyst, professor at Postgraduate Center for Mental Health: "Waiting out a bad marriage until the children are grown is not the answer. If a remarriage is a corrective, a realigning of sights, and the person has chosen a more compatible partner emotionally, then the children might fit into that second marriage comfortably. My own feeling is that sometimes the children can fit in, if the new wife is a loving woman, and accepting, and if the father doesn't use the children as some kind of pawn."

MILDRED NEWMAN AND BERNARD BERKOWITZ, analysts, coauthors of *How to Be Your Own Best Friend,* and husband and wife:

"We each have two children from our first marriages," says Mildred Newman, "and when we decided to get married, my daughter wouldn't come to the wedding, and she said she wouldn't speak to me again. She started to cry, and she cried for seven days and seven nights.

"Everyone said, 'What are you going to do about this?' And I said, 'She has to cry and I have to get married.' I truly felt that way. It took six months for her to change her attitude. I did not want to give her the responsibility of deciding whether or not I should marry."

Should a parent remarry if a child is violently opposed to it?

Accepting a child's dictation, according to Bernard Berkowitz, "is the equivalent of robbing a child of a parent, by putting this responsibility on a child's shoulders. It's your life, and your decision, and in time Mildred's daughter became one of my best friends."

"It's Like an Armed Camp"

Some, but not all, psychiatrists who work with children feel that a child should not make the decision as to which parent he or she should live with. Many lawyers contend that a teen-age child has the right to that decision, but Dr. Curran says:

"It is my personal feeling that even an adolescent should not be forced to make the decision, because if he makes the decision for his mother, he still has to see his father, and every time he sees his father, he'll feel guilt, remorse, hostility, because he's been forced to make such a decision.

"If a child expresses a desire to live with one parent or another, one should listen to him, but he should not be made to feel that he's the one who's making the decision, because he may feel that afterward his decision will be used against him by the other parent."

But what to do when a child comes to a father and says, "I don't want to live with Mommy. I want to live with you. Why can't I live with you? Don't you want me?"

This was the problem faced by a man in his late thirties, Eugene F., who was divorced and had a daughter of nine, Cindy. His wife left Chicago, where they had been living, and moved to Tucson with Cindy. The child visited her father during school holidays and vacations, and everything seemed to be working out reasonably well, until Mr. F. married a divorcee with two little boys of her own. The boys, five and seven, lived with their mother and new stepfather, and became so attached to Mr. F. that before very long they were calling him Daddy.

All this was most upsetting to Cindy when she came visiting Easter week.

"He's not your daddy," she'd shriek at the little boys. "He's mine!"

The boys, who had been brought up with exceptional permissiveness, were quick to retaliate by leaping on their stepsister and pummeling her with their fists.

"It's like an armed camp when Judy's boys and Cindy get together," said Mr. F.

But yet, when Cindy begged and begged to come and live with her father, he felt that he should acquiesce, and hired a lawyer to help him gain custody of his daughter.

"Cindy loves me," he said. "She wants to be with me. My ex-wife is a neurotic, and Cindy isn't happy with her mother. Why shouldn't she live with me if that's what she wants?"

That, of course, was what Cindy wanted, but her motives were an amalgam of some love and much jealousy when she saw her father developing a deepening relationship with his two stepsons. She had never asked to live with her father before he remarried.

The custody battle for Cindy was taken to court, and Cindy herself was questioned by the judge as to whom she wanted to live with. Cindy was put in the unfortunate position of having to choose between her parents, but she has a streak of stubborn, stick-to-itiveness, and she answered: "I want to live with my father."

The judge hearing the case was no Solomon, and he asked the little girl, "Why? Don't you love your mother?"

Cindy looked at her parents, who sat at opposite sides of the room, and she started to wail, "I love my mother, I do, but I want to live with my father."

The judge awarded Mr. F. temporary custody, and Cindy went to live with her father, stepmother, and stepbrothers. Mr. F., a sharp and shrewd businessman, considered highly knowledgeable by his friends and business competitors, was still naïve about his daughter's true motives. As the months went by, however, it became more and more evident that the little girl was hoping to separate her father as completely as possible from her stepbrothers. When Mr. F. explained that she would have to accommodate her life to the presence of the two little boys, Cindy went into what her father and step-mother termed a long sulk. But when she didn't come out of that state, they realized that her feelings were more complicated and involved than they had realized, and they took her to see a psychiatrist. The doctor explained that the child was in a seriously depressed state, and said, after seeing Cindy a few times, that she—and they—needed a great deal of help. Three years have passed, and Mr. and Mrs. F. and Cindy are each still having their own hour a week with the psychiatrist.

"It's the old 'life can be beautiful' syndrome," said an observant family counselor. "It seemed so simple to the father: why shouldn't his daughter live with him? By not taking her real motivations into consideration, and by giving in to her demand, he forced her into the position of choosing between him and his ex-wife—a choice that was bound to fill Cindy with guilt."

Cindy's mother responded to Cindy's rejection of her by acting out a rejection of Cindy. She moved to southern Mexico, and because of the expense and the difficulty of the trip, Cindy can see her mother only once a year. Today Mr. F. has permanent custody and he says:

"Cindy gets along a lot better with her stepmother than she does with me. She gets angry with me a lot, and sometimes months go by when she won't talk to me. Just won't talk. We'll all be sitting at the dinner table together and she pretends I'm not there. But she gets along fine with Judy, though it's obvious that she still hates the boys."

"She's angry with her father," explained the family counselor, "because he's the one that's important to her. I imagine that her stepmother is nothing more than a convenience person—you know, a person who does things for you, but who has no real emotional value in your life."

The only ones who seem to have remained unscathed are Judy's two sons, who so far seem to be protected from the knotted and complicated emotions about them by their own boisterous and raucous personalities.

"They yell so loud about what they want," complained Cindy, "that they can't hear what anyone else is saying."

Yes. And maybe with reason.

An interesting trend in recent years is that some young women *don't* want custody of their children when they divorce. According to a family court lawyer in a large city, "There's been a definite trend in the courts to award the child in the child's best interests; it is no longer a foregone conclusion that the mother gets the child.

"The judge determines the 'best interest' by hearing testimony from professionals—in many cases, psychiatrists. Also by interviewing the children, if they're old enough. In many instances, if the parent who wants custody is remarried, or will remarry, the judge may interview the new parent, too."

Children are sensitive. Many people recognize that, likening them with a sticky gush of analogy to small, tender buds, tiny, delicate shoots, pathetic little plants. If some believe that there are children closer to the sturdy, prickly cactus than to the shy violet hiding beneath the green leaf, they don't talk about it. Especially not in the United States, which, next to Israel, may be the only genuine "pediarchy." Children are regarded somewhat differently in Europe. Rob, a character in Rumer Godden's *The Battle of the Villa Fiorita*, made a good, strong European point when he said that his daughter ". . . knows she has to study me and find out what mood I'm in. That will teach her to deal with other people," but this is a point of view not regarded with much favor in the United States, and if some do recognize the need for getting *from,* as well as giving *to,* children, they rarely speak of it; the needs of children are supreme.

Remarriages in which both spouses arrive with children from previous marriages seem to work out better than those in which only one spouse has children. People with children of their own, when faced with stepchildren, recognize the need for accommodation.

"Now We Can Have Fresh Raspberries"

Rhonda D., a widow who married for the second time when she was in her fifties, said, "I have three children from my first marriage, and my husband has two children from his first marriage. I was always very careful, if I did something for one of my children, not to exclude my new husband. Even if it was merely providing a new delicacy. My youngest son was in college when I got married the second time, and he'd spend holidays and vacations with us, and if my husband saw me buy raspberries, for instance, he'd say, 'Oh, I see that Paul's coming home, and now we can have fresh raspberries.' He was just teasing, and these are just small things, but I was aware of them.

"And I've always made a conscious effort that the proper observations were made—you know, like my stepchildren's birthdays. My husband always sends a check, but I like to supplement that with a little nicety —something personal. When there's a holiday, I try to buy goodies.

"When it's a family get-together, I try to have all our

children there—and our children's children. There was an amusing incident one time when I gave a big family party and my grandchildren were there, and so were my husband's. Well, one of the kids wanted a special drink —he always liked a maraschino cherry in his ginger ale —and then the others wanted it, too, and when I went to get it, one of them said, 'She's my grandmother,' and another one said, 'No, she's my grandmother,' and the oldest one said, 'Well, she's the grandmother of us all.'

"So I've tried, and my husband, by the same token, tries too. For example, he gave up his den, which he loved to use for reading and watching television, and it became Paul's room when he came home from college. And because Paul is very gregarious and has many friends, there were lots of doings and lots of goings on, very much not in keeping with my husband's nature, which is quiet, and not as social as my children or I.

"He gave up his den graciously, and never said, 'I'm having to give up my room for his friends.' He did request that Paul's friends not telephone after twelve o'clock at night, so I would always disconnect the phone in our bedroom. But I think there has to be adjustment and giving up from both parties, otherwise you just can't make a go of it.

"And the inner feelings that you're partial to your own —your own children, your own grandchildren—you can't always show them. You feel them, and you do certain things that you don't necessarily communicate— I mean, finances and that sort of thing. You can do that if you work, as I do, or have money from your first marriage."

"She's Manipulative, and She Can Be Delicious"

Not all parents who remarry are as adept at hiding such inner feelings, and sometimes it becomes obvious that they think: My children are a lot better (nicer/smarter/ prettier/kinder) than your children.

Virginia P. is a divorcee with three boys from her first marriage. Her husband left her when her boys were three, six, and eight, and ten years later she married Ralph, divorced, with two college-age daughters. The three boys live with Virginia and Ralph, and conflicts do arise.

"The conflict comes where there are moral issues involved, and somehow the moral issues and the money get mixed up. Now, Ralph's younger daughter is in college. She's manipulative, and she can be delicious, but she can manipulate you into a corner—even me, but I know it and I let her, and that's all right.

"Ralph's other daughter—she's nineteen—is with a boy, Joey, in Colorado. Last week the boy's mother, who is a neighbor of ours, called and actually said to my husband, 'You are a cheap son-of-a-bitch Jew bastard. I send Joey money to Colorado, and all he has to do with his money is support your rich little Jewish princess.'

"Well, Ralph said, 'I don't have to listen to this. I didn't choose their life style for them, and I think it's wrong, and as long as I think it's wrong, I have no intention of supporting them in it.'

"Well, about an hour later the phone rings again, and it's Ralph's daughter from Colorado. She was picked up in a local dime store for lifting a can of deodorant, and she's belligerent, sullen, bitchy, until she smells that there's no way back, and then she reverses her position and becomes a smiler, and she tells her father what has happened.

"Ralph was very controlled, which made me furious, and I said, 'How can you talk to her that way, she's such a bitch. If she were my kid, I would kick her downstairs.' Ralph doesn't get mad at me when I talk that way; he just said, 'I don't know how to deal with these things.'

So I said, 'How long are you going to operate that damn guilt button? You're not guilty. And if you are guilty of what was, start fresh. She is what she is. But you've got to get her to start fresh. I'm not saying don't send money to bail her out. Send her fifty dollars—a hundred—who cares? But at least let her know how you feel.'

"So here's this thing with the fifty dollars, and it's over, right? The next morning we come down, and my youngest child, Rod, who's fifteen—who's not kind, he's super-kind: he tells fat girls they're beautiful—he comes in and says, "Ma, give me six dollars. I'm sponsoring Robin on a walk for muscular dystrophy.' You know, they sponsor them at a dollar a mile, and Robin walked six miles, and the money goes to the Muscular Dystrophy Foundation.

"And I look in my pocketbook and I don't have it, and Ralph says, 'Should I give it to him?' and I say, 'Darling, give him the six dollars.' Anyway, Rod gets the six dollars, and then Ralph and I go out to the car—we drive to work together—and Ralph says, 'You know, about that six dollars—it seems to me that if a kid wants to make a contribution to charity, it should be at some sacrifice of his own.'

"So I said, 'Ralph, I love you, but go screw yourself. Rod doesn't take an allowance. When he needs money, I give it to him; that's the way it's always been. I would have given him the six dollars if I'd had it in my purse, I would have given him twenty, because I know he's giving it to a charity, but fifty dollars to a judge to bail your daughter out—what was her sacrifice?'

"And you know what Ralph said to me a couple of days later? His daughter—the one in Colorado—promised to look for a job. Would I buy her some blouses so she could look nice when she goes to work? I wouldn't buy her shit with my money. I told Ralph, 'If you want to go shopping, go ahead, go buy her. You're nuts, where are your values?' It's his guilt again. I'm glad I waited until my kids were grown before I got married again. I never wanted anybody telling me how to raise my kids. It was much easier raising them alone. It was what I said, and that was it, or it was what we decided together. Some things that I said, no argument, and nothing democratic about it; and some things we discussed. Anyway, I have great kids, they're so kind."

"That Man, Your Father"

Dr. Norman J. Levy, commenting on the plight of many divorced fathers, says: "Most often the children remain with the mother, and the children and mother get closer, partly because the mother contributes to the estrangement by saying things like, 'That man, your father,' or 'You tell *that man,* your father . . .'

"The father feels more estranged from his children, especially if he has strong feelings for them. He misses them. Oh, sure, there are some guys who say, 'Oh, boy, I'm free,' but they may have a feeling, too, that a part of their lives has been taken away.

"Many men feel bereft. Of course, they don't like the rigid routine of having to see their children every single Saturday and Sunday, or every other weekend, or every Wednesday night. That's not natural. Parents and children don't relate that way, on schedule. They get resentful.

"But there are the holidays: Thanksgiving kind of holidays, Christmas, Jewish holidays, family occasions, family get-togethers. That's when many of these men feel bad."

The man who doesn't have custody of his children feels bad, or he feels guilty, and he feels responsible, at least in part, for his children's unhappiness. The woman who has custody feels angry and self-righteous. After all, *he* may be sending her money to help support the children, but it is *she* who has the day-to-day responsibility of bringing them up, of seeing that they brush their teeth, get to school on time, wear their boots on a snowy day. What happens to the children who are exposed to the often erratic moods of parents, and later on face new relations with stepparents?

Says Dr. Levy, "In almost all relationships, the big factors are those that involve power and control, and the claims and expectations that are based on 'if you love me.' You know: 'If you love me, you'll satisfy all my needs.' In a good marriage it's worked out equitably, so that the two people say, 'Let's understand what your needs are, and what my needs are, and we'll mutually agree to try to resolve our differences. I'll satisfy some of your needs, and you'll satisfy some of mine. I'll give up some of my needs at moments, and you'll give up some of yours, and we'll play compromise.'

"Now, when children get into the scene, even in a good marriage, you begin to get triangles, and quadrangles, and pentagons, in which each child now wants to get into the power struggle, and learns to manipulate and maneuver, and tries to get the best out of the deal, and tries to get his own needs fulfilled.

"A child knows that he's got one father and one mother, and he tries to work them against one another in his own best interests, against his brothers' and sisters' interests, and so on.

"But if there's a divorce and a remarriage, another element has been added. Children often feel that the new wife is getting things from the father that they should be getting, and they sometimes try to make a breach between the two—to get the father and to alienate the second wife. They want the father's attention, his money, his love.

"You've got that to start with. However, if the man and woman have learned something from their previous experiences, if the first divorce is not just something that ended in bitterness and acrimony—and if the children are not 'monsters'—the children can fit in.

"By 'monsters' I mean children who have been neurotically involved in their parents' marriage. If they have been so involved, they'll bring their neurotic patterns into the new marriage, and the woman will be hard put, because she has the status of a wife but none of the prerogatives of a mother—to physically punish or tell off.

"She's got to be careful, for often the husband feels guilty, knows she's right, but feels he should be on the side of his children, because he doesn't want to alienate them. He also doesn't want to alienate his new wife, but being caught in his own conflict, he tends to lash out at the person with whom he feels he can get away with it most, usually his wife. This can sometimes lead to another divorce."

It takes a strong stomach, healthy nerves, and immeasurable love to cope with the Borgia-like combination of wily, neurotic children and a father's guilt. Because children *are* wily. The best of them, at the best of times, are manipulative. Parents, working together, can check much of that. But one natural parent plus one stepparent are often not a match for a child who's out to divide, irritate, and hurt, and hopes to gain all the attention.

I found that it is stepmothers, with stepchildren who don't live with them but whom they see on a regular basis, that have the most difficulty. Customs are changing, and in some cases fathers do gain custody of their children, but most of the time they still remain in their mother's care. Thus, when stepchildren come calling, they often expect to be treated as visitors, with all of a visitor's prerogatives and none of the responsibilities that face regular members of a household.

Yet these young "visitors" are more than that. They are coming to their father's house, which in a way is their second home. And in many cases their visits do occur with some regularity.

When a man marries a woman with children who are in her custody, he becomes the father figure in that household, and takes on much of the authority of a father—the man of the house. But stepmothers balance on a shaky tightrope: they lack the authority of a mother and have few rights as disciplinarians, but certainly they are more than hostesses to children whom they see once a week, or every two weeks.

"I tried to explain my feelings once," said Mary R., married for five years and stepmother to two teen-agers, "but I never got any sympathy—not even from my close friends, who all have children of their own. I could tell that I was beginning to look like the wicked stepmother to them, until I put it this way: 'How would you feel if your mother-in-law and father-in-law came to visit you every other weekend, from Friday through Sunday, and if these visits continued year in and year out?' Well, that got to them; nobody likes their in-laws that much, and nobody had thought of stepchildren in that way."

"If My Stepchild Ever Does That Again, I'll . . ."

VIVIAN Z.: When my husband, Dave, and I first got married, his two children came to spend a week with us while their mother went to Florida. My eight-year-old stepson came bearing his own cans of tuna fish and fruit juice for the next day's school lunch.

"We have tuna and juice," I explained.

"I only want this brand," he said. "I won't eat the cheap brands you have in this house." My husband thought it was funny, but I didn't.

AUDREY R.: My stepdaughter, Patty, is bright, and knows how to say hurting things very cleverly. She goes to a special high school for bright kids, and one Friday night when she came to spend the weekend, she told us that her drama teacher had asked the class to mime their fathers' actions when they first get home at night from work.

Patty said that she acted out a scene of a man taking off his coat, his jacket, walking to the kitchen sink, and washing the dishes that had been left there. She further reported that her teacher had said, "Come on, Patty, your father doesn't do that when he comes home from work." But Patty had assured her that was just what her father did do, just about every night.

The truth is that my husband and I both work, but I'm the one who usually does the kitchen chores. Bob does help out, though, especially when the children are there, and this was Patty's acid little comment on the fact that I "made" her father do the dishes.

LOUISE W.: My stepchildren talk to me in a tone that I wouldn't use toward a maid—if I had one.

Examples? Well, there was one Saturday evening when I was setting the table for supper, and my stepdaughter, Susanna, who was then eleven, came over and said, very lady-to-servant, "Can I give you a hand with that?" As a matter of fact, if I did speak that way to a cleaning lady, she'd quit.

And I'll never forget one Thanksgiving—my husband's kids always spend four or five days with us at

Thanksgiving. Well, I was in the kitchen, cooking up a storm. You know how you do, course after course of goodies. About twelve noon, Susanna, who was fourteen then, ambled out of her room wrapped in her robe. She had just gotten out of bed. She watched me wrestle a huge turkey out of the oven to baste it. We have a small kitchen, and it gets really hot. After I got the turkey back in the oven, I looked up, and Susanna gave a bored little yawn, and said, "Is there any coffee left?"

GERRY P.: My stepson, Stephen, is the haughtiest thirteen-year-old you'll ever see. Last year we took him out to our beach cottage for the weekend. On Sunday my husband went off to play tennis, saying that he was going to take Stephen to the beach when he returned in two hours. We were invited to a barbecue later on that day, so I waited an hour, did some weeding, and then went inside to wake Stephen. He takes a long time to get up, and I wanted him to be ready to go to the beach with his father.

I woke Stephen, who mumbled something, and then I went out to the garden again. About half an hour later, I went back in, thinking to make Stephen some breakfast. He was out of bed and sitting in the living room, looking worldly and bored and staring into space. It's kind of hard to see a thirteen-year-old take up that pose.

"Stephen," I said, "how about some breakfast?"

"No," he said, "I'm not ready for that just yet."

I went back to the garden, and said the hell with him, let his father make his breakfast. Do you think the kid came out to see what I was doing, or to offer me a hand, or even to ask for breakfast? No, he just sat there, bored, I'm sure, but waiting to be waited on by his father. My husband does have a picture of Stephen looking like

Gainsborough's "Blue Boy," and that's how he acts—
like a little spoiled prince.

MADY C.: I suppose the worst thing is that my husband
doesn't *see* what his children do. My stepdaughter, Corinne, tends to get up around one on the weekends she
spends with us. One Saturday I fixed lunch for my husband and my stepson, and they were just about to eat
when Corinne finally got up and came out to the dining
room.

My husband was instantly on his feet. "Do you want
something to eat?" he asked Corinne. "Yes," she said,
"that looks good." He was about to give her his plate, his
silverware, and his napkin. I couldn't help it—I came
charging out of the kitchen.

"Corinne is sixteen," I said. "I think she's old enough
to come out to the kitchen and help herself."

My husband was angry with me when the weekend
was over. "I wouldn't have noticed that," he said, "if you
hadn't made a fuss. Why don't you just go away when
the children come? Go somewhere." If I didn't love him
so much, I guess I *would* go away—for good.

Parents overreact to criticism of their children, and
stepparents overreact to evidence of bad manners and
insensitivity on the part of their stepchildren. Fathers
react because they feel guilty, and stepmothers react
because they know that they've placed themselves in a
situation in which they will never be first, never be the
one most loved.

It helps when both parents and stepparents recognize
that in a divorce, children often ricochet from parent to
parent, picking up angers and antagonisms as they go.
They cannot help but react to the moods and tempers
that surround them. It's all very well to claim, "I never
say anything against my ex," but it takes an unusually

noble character not to slip in a slight hint or innuendo about *"That man,* your father," or *"That woman,* your mother."

Children are made up of more complex ingredients than sugar, spice, and puppy-dog tails. They are also combinations of heredity, environment, and upbringing. Over the past years, with the increased emphasis on permissiveness, many children are allowed wide latitudes of behavior—frequently bad. It's not only stepchildren who present a sorry picture of rudeness, insensitivity, and a lack of respect toward others. Children with two happily married parents can be just as difficult. The difference is that parents who stay together can present a more strongly united front when it comes to coping with their children, and there are no stepparents around to carry tales.

"I was complaining to a friend of mine once," said Doreen J., a recently married woman in Ann Arbor with three stepchildren, "and he just said, 'Well, you knew what the cards were when they were dealt. You didn't have to pick them up.'

"Sure, I did know, but I couldn't know how my husband's kids would really be—could I?"

"I Did Think Things Would Change"

The not really knowing extends to the parents as well as to stepparents. As one father in San Francisco said, "I did think things would change in time. Well, I was wrong. My kids just don't see my wife as anything—as a person—as someone important to me. As a matter of fact, my daughter, who's fourteen, still thinks of her mother as my wife. I know she feels that way because this summer, when she wanted me to take her away for the weekend and I wouldn't, she actually said, 'If you don't take me, I know something that I can tell Mommy about you—and I will.' At first I was just furious that she had the nerve to threaten me, and then I realized that she was threatening me with her mother—who was no longer my wife. My daughter still felt that her mother was a lot more important to me than my present wife."

The conflict frequently enlarges so that it's father and child against the new wife. It's a battle in which everyone is the loser, especially since the husband's actions are motivated as much by guilt as by love, and the guilt he feels about his children is soon compounded by the guilt he feels toward his current wife.

One Philadelphia man made an unusual decision. He was divorced, and his four children were in his ex-wife's custody. About a year after his divorce he remarried, and shortly after that, his first wife died. Usually, in such cases, the children come to live with their father, but this man sent his children to live with his ex-wife's sister.

"I knew my marriage would never last if my kids came to live with us. It was a hard decision, but I had to make it. My kids are very hostile to my wife, and I knew she'd be unable to handle them.

"Believe me, I love my kids, but I had to make this choice. It involved the rest of my life. After all, kids do grow up and leave you, but I hope to be married to my present wife as long as I live."

One scene that occurs in many remarriages is the "let's all get into bed with Daddy" bit. Anne Dowie of San Francisco, telling in *Harper's Weekly* about her trials with her stepchildren, remembers walking into her bedroom and finding her husband, his four children, and their ninety-pound dog all in bed together.

A stepmother in Boston said that she could understand the psychological reasons why her stepdaughter tried to get into the bed she shared with her husband.

"She was always terribly jealous of me; I suppose she would have felt that way about her own mother if her parents hadn't divorced. I remember when we were first married, and the kids came to spend their first weekend with us. I got up on Saturday morning, opened the door, and Joanie fell into the room. She had been sitting on the floor, her back against the door, for I don't know how long.

"That was seven years ago, and Joanie is sixteen and over it, but Martin still wants to get into bed with Daddy —and he's fourteen. If my husband lies down for a nap, Martin lies down with him, whether it's on the couch, the chaise, or in our bed."

It's a wise stepparent who realizes that certain types of behavior would be manifested whether it's a natural parent or a stepparent that's involved. This stepmother understood that at some stage, many little girls become very jealous of their mothers vis-à-vis their fathers. What Joanie resented was her stepmother's relationship to her father and if Joanie's parents had remained married to each other, Joanie probably would have felt similarly about her own mother.

Many people who remarry are afraid to behave affectionately toward each other when stepchildren are around. Wrong, says child psychiatrist Dr. J. Louise Despert. "The child has to *see* the affection. Show affection for each other even if it is initially upsetting to the child."

Seeing that a parent cares for a new spouse is one way a child can learn to face up to reality. A remarriage founded on love can withstand a lot of pressures, especially when husband and wife are willing to face the sad fact that some children have neurotic needs that may be inimical to the healthy needs of the parents.

"Love me, love my child," as the old saying goes, and the best that anyone can answer is, "I'll try."

Of course, in a remarriage where the children are grown and out of the house, the chances of conflict are minimized—but not completely so.

A Connecticut widower with three older children married a highly successful executive in an important New York advertising agency.

"I didn't have any trouble with my husband's seventeen-year-old son," she said, "even though he lived with us, but it was my stepdaughters—twenty-one and twenty-three—who gave me a lot of trouble. The oldest was married, but she divorced shortly after my husband and I got married, and while she didn't come home to live, she demanded constant attention and help from my husband. I mean emotional and financial help. It was as though she couldn't bear not being Daddy's girl. I think that's really why she got divorced. I'm just surprised that she ever got married."

With all the problems that reverberated around her stepdaughters, is this woman still married? Yes, she is, as are almost all the people interviewed for this book.

At the beginning of each interview, the same question was asked: "What are the biggest problems you have in your remarriage?"

And the answer would come: "Children and money," or "Money and children," but where the relationship was based on something more than the need to have the outer trappings or the status of marriage, the marriage survives.

In marriages where both partners have children from previous marriages, there's a lot more understanding and giving on both sides. And even if the understanding does not stem from true affection for the children, and is not always completely sincere, there is at least a recognition of the practical politics of the situation, as in:

"You do for my children, and I'll do for yours."

This may not be in the best tradition of marriages made in heaven, but there is a realism here that works far better than the wide-eyed approach of: "I just know I'm going to love your children because they're yours."

Of course they are *his,* or *hers,* but they are also one half of *the other*—that person who is no longer loved, but who exercises a strong influence on the children, and on the remarriage.

Not all stories about stepchildren are horror stories. Some children are open and accepting of new relationships. They reach out, and are enriched by the extra loving they receive in return.

"My Stepdaughter Is Closer to Me Than My Own Daughter"

MARSHA A.: I was twenty-three when I got married the first time, and my husband, Kevin, was a lot older than I, and he had been married before and had two children. When I met him, the two children were living with his mother, and he was also living with his mother. She was quite wealthy; they had a very beautiful setup, complete with nurse, and all kinds of things that his mother needed to take care of the children.

My husband's first wife—this sounds silly as the dickens—but his wife ran away with his best friend, who was also his business partner. The little girl was about six, and the little boy around four, and Kevin's mother adored having them. All mama wanted was to keep the whole family all together and she never, never, never wanted Kevin baby to get married again.

But we met and fell in love, and got married, and at that point I certainly was not capable of taking over two children. And then we had a daughter of our own, and my husband adored her, and the other two children were shunted around between grandparents.

I had my stepson, Donal, from the time he was four, but I did not have Sally until she was fourteen, because she was living with her maternal grandparents. And fourteen is a hard age to take over a child; actually, we never felt like mother and daughter. She called me Marsha. I tried to establish some kind of discipline, but she resented everything.

But you know, strangely enough, as the years went by, this adorable, darling stepdaughter of mine became closer to me than my own blood daughter. My first husband died, and I'm remarried, and my second husband and I go to Vermont every Thanksgiving, and we spend that holiday with Sally and her family.

I guess the turning point came for me and Sally when she got married and had a baby. Her father disliked and disapproved of the man she married, and he did not want to go to the wedding, and he said, "If you go to the wedding, you'll be going against me," so I didn't go, but I wanted to very much, and Sally knew I was for her. And today, here is my second husband, Stuart, and we spend every Thanksgiving with Sally and her family, and Stuart and I both adore them.

And we have the greatest time in the world with them, and now Sally has her own daughter growing up and getting married, and everything, and it's like my granddaughter. Sally is my real, real daughter—not my blood daughter.

As for my own daughter, I haven't seen her for two years, even though we do speak on the phone. This is her life style, but Sally and I are so close, and I love her so dearly, and yet we had such antagonisms, such battles. But she outgrew it, and I outgrew it, and today I just absolutely adore her.

I'm sorry to say I don't see Donal, but he married the most terrible person you can ever imagine, and even Sally, his own sister, hasn't seen or spoken to him in at least ten years. But me and Sally, well, it's wonderful.

"Gee, Man, I Really Gave You a Hard Time"

HANNAH S.: Frank and I have a special marriage, an interracial marriage. When we got married, my first husband's mother—my ex-mother-in-law—did a lot of damage there. She was so angry that I was involved with a black man, and although they are the best liberals, and always have been, all their deep-rooted prejudices seemed to come out that I dared to marry a black man.

The influence on my son, Charles, was very negative, so that Charles's very important years from ten to fifteen were a tremendous struggle. During that time, my son lived mostly with my ex-mother-in-law; it was a voluntary arrangement that we made, an unusual situation. My first husband and I agreed to have our son live on so-called neutral ground.

Frank had a lot to deal with when it came to Charles, but he is a unique human being. He has tremendous depth about how people feel about prejudice. Not about him personally, but the whole picture of prejudice. He understood it, and he handled it very well. He never applied pressure on Charles, but he never withdrew either.

It was a hard struggle, and I take some of the credit for the results, because it was a battle, and there were nights when I was climbing the walls. Nobody knew it, but I wouldn't break down, and I wouldn't give in. You need time and patience to let things fall into place very naturally.

Because I knew that Charles, after a while . . . I just

knew that Charles could do nothing but end up loving Frank. In fact, everything came to fruition. About a year or two ago, Charles was having dinner with us—he was around nineteen when this happened, and Frank and I had been married about ten years—well, he was having dinner with us, and Frank and Charles were talking about something, and I heard Charles say to Frank, "Gee, man, I really gave you a hard time in those days, didn't I?" And it was Charles's way of saying, I'm sorry. I had to go into the other room, because I was crying. I knew then that Charles had become a man, if he could say that to Frank. I look at them today and I can see that Charles and Frank are more alike than Charles and my first husband.

"Her Daughter Knew My Daughter—That's How We Met"

BARTON D.: My children were about thirteen and fifteen when I married Margo, and they weren't living with me, but I saw them, we had a good relationship. You can have a good relationship without living together every day, and they were very pleased when I told them I was marrying Margo. Besides, Margo always made it warm and pleasant for my kids, they never felt left out. Margo's daughter knew my daughter—that's how we met.

I was in East Hampton with the kids, and my daughter said she wanted to look up an old school friend. Coincidentally, a few months before I had been talking to some friends about looking for a house to rent in East Hampton, and they said, "Well, if you're out there, look up Margo C., she's been out there for years," and it turned out that Margo's daughter was my daughter's friend, and when I went over with my daughter one Sunday morning and met Margo, that was it. I walked away, and

I said, I'm going to marry that woman, and about five months later we were married.

MARGO D.: My kids were thirteen, eighteen, and twenty when Bart and I got married, and they were delighted, they like Bart very much. There was no problem, they never gave any indication of being unhappy. I think they were sincere, and they love Bart.

My youngest child—my daughter—she was a difficult and impossible child, but not because of our marriage, I think. Possibly because of what came before. But she was difficult, seriously so, and she had serious psychological problems, and was hospitalized for ten months, and Bart was incredible. He was much more a father to her than her own father; he was marvelous through it. And my daughter has been living with us until just about a year and a half ago, when she started college, and she always comes home to us—and it really is to *us*. Bart's children do call me the "mean old stepmother"—but that's our family joke.

"We All Spend Holidays Together"

JASON V.: I have four children from my first marriage, and my wife has two children from her first marriage, and we had to solve problems like what do you do about Passover? So we have the first night's seder at my house, and my first wife and all the kids come. For the second night we go to my first wife's house—this includes my second wife and her two kids—so that we spend both holiday evenings together. There are no problems. My first wife and my second wife are friends. I like my stepchildren—they live with us—and my children like my wife, and they like to be with her. This is a completely personal experience, so I don't know whether it has any

weight. I have observed this kind of situation very sel-
dom professionally [Jason is a matrimonial lawyer], so I
don't know how widespread it is, but this is how it is with
us.

"We've Worked at It"

EDWINA F.: My two stepdaughters and I have an incredi-
bly good relationship, but we've worked at it. The girls
are now eleven and fourteen, and Perry, my husband,
handled it so well with them.

At first they got a lot of negative stuff on me, as is only
natural. I didn't know their mother, and Perry said to
them, "You know, I love Edwina very much, but that
doesn't mean you have to love Edwina very much. I'm
just asking you to do this: just know that the things your
mother has told you about Edwina are very natural for
her to tell you, but she's never met Edwina; and if she
has met her, she doesn't really know her . . . she's giving
you an emotional reaction. So just be objective when you
meet Edwina, and if you don't like her, that's okay with
me, but if you do like her, don't feel embarrassed about
it."

The girls were eight and eleven when I met them, but
this was after we were married awhile. I didn't want to
challenge the situation. But now we see them one day
each weekend; they don't sleep over because we don't
have the room. They love to come over, and they love
our baby—she's eight months old—but Perry handles
these things so well. Before we actually told them that
we were going to have a child, we let them know we were
hoping to have one.

The way Perry finally worked it was to say, "Are you
partial to these names? Because if and when we have a
child, here are the names we're thinking of," and all of

a sudden, in the middle of the whole thing—with a lot of "Yes, I like that" and "No, I don't like that"—the older one looked up and said, "You're going to have a baby, aren't you?" And that was great, because they realized it themselves, and we said, "Would you like us to?" And they said, "Yes," and that was great, and then we made them part of the whole thing. So much so, that when I was taking natural childbirth classes, they'd be down on the floor doing exercises with me.

So they felt so much a part of it, and I told them that it was going to be a girl, and we picked out a name, and they began talking to her, and they would say, "Hi, Jill," and "Goodbye, Jill," and I drew the line at the little one kissing my stomach—you know, kissing Jill—which the little one wanted to do all the time.

I took them along with me to buy everything, and we were at Nieman's, and the little one, Francine, loved baby dresses, and she knew it was going to be a girl, and she knew the girl's name was going to be Jill. She also knew that the baby had turned in the birth position, I kept them aware of everything, but if you can imagine that you're at Nieman-Marcus shopping—and Francine with the dresses, kept running up to my stomach, and holding the dress upside down, and saying, "Do you like this one, Jill? Do you like this one, Jill?"

And I paid no attention, because I was used to this, but just as we were about to leave, the saleswoman came up to me and said, "You know, you have had this whole department charmed and confused. Everything has stopped for the last twenty minutes, because everyone is watching you."

People tell me we've had an unusual relationship, and I give Perry the credit, because early on, I loved them and I wanted very much for them to love me, but I was so resentful of their mother saying bad things about me that I said to Perry, "Why don't you go back and tell her that I'm a fine person, that I'm not a bad person." Perry answered, "But this is the only balm for her ego—to say that you're terrible—and if I go back and challenge her, what good does it do? Does it help the children?"

From the very beginning Perry planned things. We went to see a child psychiatrist together, which was a very good idea, and we told him that Perry wanted to leave his wife, but was this a bad time for the children, and the doctor said, "I think if they were already in their teens it would be more of a problem, and I think this is a very good time. From what I can gather, the home situation is not very pleasant, and it would be helping them if you just got the thing out into the open."

Another interesting thing, which surprised us, I had thought that first you say, "Your mother and I don't love each other," and then later you say, "I met someone else whom I want to marry." I thought that you don't say, "Your mother and I don't love each other, and by the way, I'm getting married."

But the doctor said, "No, tell them all at one time, because it's better to be honest with them, and particularly because they are little girls." This was interesting to me, but the doctor said, "Little girls worry about daddy, and who's going to take care of daddy, who's going to cook for him. If they know that daddy is going to be happy and taken care of, that is good."

I was very apprehensive, but when Perry talked to them about it, the very question Francine asked—she's very savvy—was: "Are you going to have a baby?" And Perry said, "Probably, some day," and they accepted it.

Perry is very wise. He's just appalled at some fathers. He feels that his children are just as much his children as our baby is his child, and that their welfare comes before anything else in his life except me and our baby.

The children call me Edwina, and that's a very interesting thing, too. They're very well brought up, and they always were taught to call adults Mr. and Mrs., and they never called adults by their first name. So Perry and I decided that I could become somebody extremely special if they called me Edwina, and it just works out beautifully. They still call everybody Mr. and Mrs., and they call me Edwina—Daddy and Edwina.

And they love the baby more than if they were her sisters living there all the time. They just treasure her. They never say, "This is my half-sister," but "This is my sister." If we go to a strange place and people start referring to me as their mother, I think we all tacitly agree to let it go. There's no point in saying, "This is not my mother, this is my stepmother." But with Jill—this is really their sister.

I think with stepchildren—with everybody—you have to work at it. I think you always have to be aware of not hurting people. We always put it on that basis.

And it's not always easy. Sometimes there are school plays, and Perry's ex-wife takes a stand, and says that if I come, she won't come, and the children would have to choose, but Perry makes the decision. If it is something that would be just devastating to the children not to have her there, I don't go, but if Perry feels that it's a big assembly, and no big deal, just to make a point, I do go.

And the girls often bring their friends over to our house, and we do screwy things together. Dina loves chocolate chip cookies, so for her birthday—I knew she had a regular cake at home—I doubled the chocolate chip cookie recipe, and made her one giant cookie.

Perry and I told Francine and Dina that when they go home, they don't have to make a big fuss about what we do together, by saying to their mother, "Edwina gave me this," or "Edwina cooked this for me," and they said,

"But what if she asks—shall we tell the truth?" And we said, "Yes. If she asks specific questions, always tell the truth. It's just not necessary to hurt your mother's feelings, and just know that every time you say you love Edwina, you're going to hurt her feelings."

You know, they are just so in love with the baby that they come to visit her while I'm at work. I'm really happy about that. We're so happy, we just say every day that we can't get over how marvelous things are. I know there are going to be problems. . . . I think you have to work at it.

"My Son Got Married the Same Year I Remarried"

KATHY M.: I remember just how my son reacted when I told him that I was going to marry Fred. I picked him up at the plane when he was coming home from college, and I said, "I've been dating Fred M.," and my son said, "Fine, I think he's great." I had been widowed about six years by then, and there were no children living at home for either Fred or me, but I remember distinctly that when I told him I was dating Fred, he said how fond he was of Fred. Coincidentally my son married the same year that Fred and I married. It was all very simple.

"Joe Loved My Son Almost From the Beginning"

CAROL A.: I was divorced when my son was a baby, and I started going out with Joe when Richard was about three, and Joe just sort of fell in love with my son almost from the beginning. Richard has had this eye operation, and he can only see with one eye, and he desperately wanted to play ball when he was about eight, so Joe covered one of his eyes with a bandage to see how it was, and he practiced, and he taught Richard how to pitch and hit and everything, and Richard made the team. We've been married close to nine years, and Richard rarely sees his father—*Joe* is his father. No, Joe and I don't have any of our own children. Richard is enough for us.

"He Becomes Their Ally"

HEDDA Z.: My second husband—it's very interesting— when I really lose control of myself and become emotionally buggy, he becomes my son's ally. "Take her upstairs," he says, "and lock her in her room; she's off the wall." And he's very supportive, and he talks to them about things I don't talk to them about.

Another thing that's really marvelous. Godfrey was an only child with overprotective parents. He was fifteen when he went to college, and he never lived home again, so as a result he doesn't know how to be a physical person. And my boys, they kiss a lot, so you ought to see how my son—this big, six-foot kid—puts his arm around Godfrey and gives him a kiss on top of his head, and says, "Tell me, Pop-o, were you always the shortest guy in your class?"

I came to my second marriage with a ready-made family, and I've made Godfrey much richer for it.

"I Began to Think She Was Really Okay"

LARRY G. (a twenty-eight-year-old stepson):

I know I made my stepmother's life miserable. When I think of some of the things I did! The sulks, the "I'm going to run away from home" bit—I was pretty vocal about the way I felt.

Well, the years went by. When did I realize that there was nothing hateful about my stepmother? I can't tell you the exact date or time, but it did happen. First I began to think that she was really okay, and then I began to understand that she had to be more than just okay to have put up with me all those years.

I tried to tell her how I felt, but I never could put it into words, and then I got married and my firm sent me down to Brazil. I wrote her from there, and I said, "I don't think I could be so happy today if I hadn't learned about love and understanding and forgiveness from you."

IV

The Wife Who Won't Let Go

"Every time my ex-wife has the slightest problem with our son, Joe—like when he won't eat his peas—she calls to discuss it with me."

Alexander D., New Jersey

"I take my kids out to dinner every Wednesday night, and whenever I go to pick them up, there's my ex-wife, lying on the couch in a low-cut negligee."

Bob K., New York

"His ex-wife acts as though I'm his secretary instead of his second wife. Last week she even said, 'Now you have two wives to fetch and carry for you.' And all my husband could do was to remind her that she was no longer his wife."

Patricia R., Oklahoma

That nice judge—in your home state, or perhaps in the Dominican Republic—clapped his gavel down on the round wooden disk placed before him and declared that you were, indeed, divorced.

As you walked from the courtroom, your lawyer put his hand on your shoulder and said, "It's all over."

Your Aunt Matilda in Cincinnati called your Uncle

Joe in Buffalo and told him that she doesn't know if you did the right thing, but right or wrong, you're divorced.

The people in your office were especially solicitous for about four days, and one of the men you lunch with frequently said, "Look, these things are tough, but if you weren't getting along, it's all for the best."

The lawyer, your family, business associates, and friends—they all understand that you're divorced. There's only one person who doesn't see it that way— your ex-wife.

There's nothing like the presence of an ex-wife to wreak havoc with a subsequent marriage. If there are children, they present the perfect excuse for phone calls and frequent personal conferences.

If a woman who was a wife is now an ex-wife, and hasn't remarried, she may take out all her frustrations— sexual and otherwise—on her ex-husband.

As one man put it, "Whenever my first wife is upset or annoyed—whether it's with her boyfriend or her dentist—I hear about it."

The dangers to a remarriage are apparent, but the ex-wife is also damaging herself. While she remains so involved with her ex-husband, she does not give enough time and thought to her own possibilities of remarriage.

Some women do remarry, but still insist on maintaining a strong and unhealthy relationship with their ex-husbands. They are the wives who so bitterly resent the divorce that they want to act as reminders of guilt to their ex-husbands.

In a short story aptly called "Life Sentence," Rebecca West describes a couple who meet some years after their divorce. Each has remarried, and seems to be happy, and when they meet again they launch into a furious quarrel.

" 'You're so hard I want to kill you, Josie.' " Corrie says to his ex-wife, and she responds:

" 'I wouldn't mind being killed if they got you for it.' "

The quarrel continues, with both of them shouting, until Corrie realizes that he has to leave to catch the train that will take him home. When Josie and Corrie understand that it's time to part and return to their spouses, they stop shouting. Seconds later, Josie bursts into tears, and Corrie takes her into his arms and says:

" 'Ten minutes; we've only got ten minutes. Josie, how are we going to bear this?'

"They rocked together, body to body, and looked into the years ahead."

Corrie and Josie were divorced legally, but neither was divorced emotionally. In much the same way, many women (and men, too, as you'll see in a later chapter) understand intellectually that they are, indeed, legally divorced; they have seen, and maybe even read, and certainly signed the papers to prove it, but in many cases they're not able to accept the reality of a divorce emotionally. This is especially true, explained a busy matrimonial lawyer, when the husband has initiated the divorce action.

"Many women go through with a divorce, but all the time they're thinking: He'll come back. I know he'll come back. When the husband is serious about his divorce and doesn't return to his ex-wife, she very often reacts with fury, followed by the irrational decision to *get him back*. She may no longer love him, but her sense of possession—of ownership—overrides her sense of reason.

"A woman like that—a woman who won't let go—has many weapons available to her, and she won't hesitate to use most of them. Remember Medea."

The princess Medea, in Greek mythology, was the archetype of a rejected wife whose vindictiveness is boundless. Abandoned by her husband, Jason, she avenged herself by killing their children.

Not all divorced women are wives who won't let go, and even the ones who are certainly won't act as extremely as Medea—unless they're certifiably mad—but they have other weapons that they use unhesitatingly. What are they? According to the same lawyer, the important weapons a woman will use against her estranged husband are:

Children
Guilt
Money
A combination of children and money
More guilt

The list is short, but powerful, and as one divorced man in Detroit pointed out, the emphasis on guilt is strong.

"The major factor is guilt. Absolutely. Especially if you have kids."

"My Wife Had Kept Our Apartment"

An advertising executive in New York felt that the combination of children and money was the heaviest weapon at the command of his ex-wife, and the way she wielded that weapon did result in his feeling guilty.

"When I left my first wife," he said, "she had it written into our separation agreement that the children would spend alternate weekends with me. The weekends began promptly at 7 P.M. on Friday, and were to end at 6 P.M. on Sunday—not a minute sooner. In addition to the weekends, I also spent alternate Saturdays with my kids.

"I love Donny and Gemma, and I really wanted to be with them, but you should have seen the apartment I had at the time! My wife had kept our apartment, our furniture, our books, our hi-fi stereo set, and I had left with one suitcase and the clothes on my back.

"After support payments, all I could afford was a dingy two-room walkup in the East Thirties. I furnished it with Salvation Army castoffs and dime-store dishes, and this is where my kids came on Friday nights."

The man still remembers the wife's small smile of satisfaction that first weekend when she brought Donny and Gemma to stay with their father. He also remembers his kids' reaction to their father's apartment, a place much different from their own home.

"The kids were too young to be cooped up in a tiny apartment. When the weather was nice we went for walks, to the zoo, and I must've hit every museum in town. Then there were the Saturday-afternoon kiddie movies—sometimes I used to sneak out to a nearby bar for a fast martini."

Donny, explained his father, had a quality of childish honesty that was most appealing.

"I still remember taking my kids to a Christmas performance of the *Nutcracker* ballet, and about half-way through, Donny piped up, 'It's too long!' I laughed, and so did a lot of parents around me, because Donny had said what a lot of them must have been thinking.

"Well, one day he looked around my apartment and said, 'This is a terrible place! Why don't you come home with me and Gemma?' Donny was being honest; it *was* a terrible place and it made it even harder for him to understand why I had left him, his sister, their mother —and a comfortable home. I had to try to explain all over again, and there were tears, and Donny asking, 'You mean you want to stay here?'

"My wife—we were only separated at that point—had put me in the position of having to make painful explanations once again. I guess she thought that maybe rather than do that, I'd go back to her—but I didn't."

Obviously, it wasn't only the need for explanation that the wife was counting on to drive the man back to her. She was using a great many weapons simultaneously; insisting that her separated husband care for the children on alternate weekends and Saturdays was meant to remind him of his responsibilities to her and their children. Then, too, a man whose children occupy so much of his free time doesn't have many hours left to become involved with other women.

And should he, somehow, manage to become interested in someone else, the children are there to act as reminders that this man has made a large prior commitment—a discouraging note to a woman who wants a home and a family of her own.

"You'd Think She'd Give Up"

Arnold D., another ex-husband whose children visited with him on alternate weekends, said that if he couldn't stick to his ex-wife's rigidly maintained schedule, she insisted that he "make up" any weekend he might have skipped, by having his children visit him an extra weekend at another time.

Mr. D. loved his children and wanted to be with them, but two weekends in a row created a large strain in his remarriage, because his children and his second wife shared, at best, an armed truce. His ex-wife also insisted that their children come visiting even when they weren't feeling completely well. The every-other-weekend, plus "make-up" weekends, went on for better than seven years—until the children were in their teens and began to have their own weekend plans.

Was the first Mrs. D. a strange, unloving mother; was she a "monster"? Not really; for the most part, she was a loving, concerned mother, but she was also a woman in the grip of a compulsion. She had considered her marriage to Mr. D. much the same as one would consider a business transaction. She gave birth to their children, cared for them and the home; Arnold D. was expected to fulfill the role of breadwinner, father, and husband/lover, in that order. If Arnold didn't live up to his wife's expectations of him as a moneymaker, she'd rage, and get even by not observing all the clauses of their unwritten marriage contract. She'd avoid entertaining his friends or business associates whenever possible, and she'd be noncommunicative both verbally and sexually.

You do for me, and I'll do for you—those were the unspoken, unwritten, yet very concrete terms of the marriage contract as Mrs. D. saw it. If they had been inscribed on a tablet of stone, they wouldn't have been more real to her.

Arnold D.'s defection from their marriage, and his subsequent remarriage, did not abrogate that unwritten agreement, in her eyes. They had made a deal, and one way or another, Mrs. D. was determined to make Arnold D. live up to its terms.

"We were married for ten years," Arnold D. said, "but we've been divorced for almost that long. You'd think she'd give up."

But often a compulsive person can't give up—not unless she is helped toward her own release by a professional therapist. By working out her own problems and examining her background, she might come to see what went wrong in terms of what she herself contributed to the souring of the marriage.

"Women who won't let go have many devices," says Dr. Norman J. Levy. "Say a father was supposed to have the kids visit him on Memorial Day weekend, but instead he's planned to go on a vacation or a business trip at that time, so he tells his ex-wife that he can't see the kids that weekend. Then there's a big hassle, and the mother says to the kids, 'Your father won't take you; he doesn't want to be with you,' and then they feel bad, and the father feels terrible."

According to a recent study on divorce conducted by a group of lawyers, there's been an interesting change in the attitudes and behavior pattern of divorced women with children.

"Years ago," said a member of the bar, "a woman would try to get back at her ex-husband by denying him the right to see their children. I went through plenty of court fights, trying to obtain visitation rights for divorced fathers.

"Today you don't see that quite as much. As a matter of fact, there's been a swing in the opposite direction, with women insisting that their ex-husbands take the children for specified lengths of time—vacations, weekends, holidays—that sort of thing."

"It's only right," said Linda F., of Maryland, thirty years old and divorced for three years. "Why should my ex-husband have all the fun and freedom? I love my two little girls, but I feel tied down if they're always with me. I expect Jeff to take the kids for some weekends. This year he even said he wants them for the month of July, and I said, 'Fine.' My mother was shocked."

"Why Wednesday?"

Another interesting pattern observed by matrimonial lawyers throughout the country is the habit of Wednesday-night dinner with the kids.

"I don't know how it got to be Wednesday night," a Detroit lawyer, himself divorced, said, "but I've been to conventions and meetings of members of the bar, and we've compared notes. Many divorced fathers are expected to take their children to dinner every Wednesday night. This is in addition to weekend visits. Why Wednesday? I guess because it's in the middle of the week. And is it common throughout the country? It sure is. I sometimes think that divorced women must have a special underground press that they use for communication. Or maybe they use smoke signals. I don't know."

Many men accept the idea of Wednesday-night dinners with the kids as a great idea—at first.

"I thought my ex-wife was terrific when she told me that she wanted me to take the kids out to supper every Wednesday," said Charles M., from Baltimore. "I mean, you hear all those terrible stories about women who won't let their ex-husbands even see their kids. But as time went by—and I mean years—I realized that she was really trying to punish me. To make me do something every Wednesday. That was one night when she knew exactly where I'd be.

"And the schedule was never allowed to change. Like one Wednesday my daughter, Elizabeth, had a cold and a slight fever, and couldn't go out for dinner. My wife called me at the office and told me to bring supper in to Elizabeth.

" 'It's Wednesday,' she said, 'and it's your turn. I'm not going to cook.' I asked her if it wouldn't be simpler to open a can of soup for Elizabeth, but she just kept repeating 'It's Wednesday,' so finally I stopped at a take-out place and bought a bucket of chicken.

"Let me tell you, though, it wasn't any fun sitting in my ex-wife's apartment while I tried to feed twelve-year-old Elizabeth chicken she was too sick to enjoy."

If a woman decides to use her children as a weapon to remind a man that he is a defector from their life together, it's a weapon she can use with great frequency because children in a household are a daily event. The divorced or separated father can be the recipient of calls, notes, visits, many of them dealing with trifles, but all meant to remind him of his duty and his connection with his ex, who is, as the old saw, and frequently the former wife, puts it, "The mother of your children."

A number of divorced men listed some of the reasons their ex-wives called them in regard to their children:

"Johnny won't eat his peas."

"Sally fights with everybody in school. I don't know what to do."

"I think Vic is failing math this year. Maybe you'd better talk to his grade adviser."

"Jane says she will not go back to Camp Runamuck. I don't know what I'm going to do with her this summer."

"Pete doesn't practice the piano."

"Joey isn't doing his homework."

As one Boston restaurateur put it, "It's not that I'm not interested in my kids—of course I am. But my business day is almost twenty-four hours long—always has been. My ex-wife never consulted me that much about the kids when we were living together; now it seems she's on the phone constantly."

And a man in San Francisco remarked, "I followed through on every one of my wife's calls about our kids. I saw my son's grade adviser, tried to choose a different camp for my daughter. With what result? My wife wouldn't listen to me *or* the grade adviser, and had my son put in a different class. She found a camp for my daughter, saying my choice of camps was terrible. She didn't really want my help or advice; she just wanted to involve me in unnecessary effort."

"I Don't Ever Have to Listen to You Again"

Asking for advice and then not taking it is a familiar device used by wives who won't let go. George H., married for the second time and living in Texas, related that his ex-wife called, very disturbed, to say that she was worried about their daughter, Bonnie, sixteen.

"I'm afraid Bonnie is having a nervous breakdown," the first Mrs. H. said. "I've just learned that she's been seeing the guidance counselor at school almost daily. She's lost a lot of weight, and he thinks she may have anorexia nervosa. Besides that, she got so hysterical during her math final that she had to be taken from the classroom. And we were all supposed to go to Austin for the weekend, and now Bonnie won't come. She says she wants to stay home all by herself, but I'm afraid to leave her alone. I just don't know what to do."

Mr. H., a concerned parent, swung into action. He called the guidance counselor, who said that Bonnie could use some therapy, though he didn't think she had anorexia nervosa and had never said so to her mother. He did say that Bonnie had been cutting her math class for months, and she had gotten so hysterical on the day of the final that she had to be taken to her family doctor.

Mr. H. then called the family doctor, and called, and called, before he finally managed to reach him. The doctor advised that it was a case of nerves, and that there was nothing seriously wrong with Bonnie.

Mr. H. then told his wife that he wanted to take Bonnie along for a weekend at their country cabin, so that he could talk to her with some amount of leisure and privacy. The second Mrs. H. agreed that it was probably a good idea, but when she approached Bonnie with the idea, the girl said that she had no wish to spend the

weekend with either her mother or her father, and she
wanted to be left alone at home. Mrs. H. backed away.
"I just didn't want to get between Bonnie, her mother,
and her father," she said.

Mr. H. didn't say anything immediately. "I knew Bonnie still had a French final to get through, and I didn't
want to upset her, but I did ask her to stop by my office
after her finals were over, so that we could talk.

"She came by one afternoon, and I told her how concerned I was, how worried about her, and how much I
loved her. That it was for all those reasons that I wanted
her to come away with us on the weekend, so that we
could talk and try to find out what was bothering her.

"Bonnie answered me with, 'I won't accept that! I
don't accept that you love me. Because if you loved me
you wouldn't make me so mad—you'd let me do what
I want. Besides, Mom says it's okay if I stay alone. She
said it was up to you. It's you who won't let me do what
I want!'

"So there I was," said Mr. H., "playing the heavy. My
ex-wife had been calling me constantly over the past few
days, asking for my help, saying she was helpless and
didn't know how to cope with Bonnie, but the moment
I stepped in, she made it clear that she hadn't really
wanted my help at all. It was just her way of dumping
on me.

"It was a familiar pattern, I realized later on, and it
was one of the very reasons I had left her. I spoke to her
on the phone later that same day, and I told her just what
I thought of her. I told her to go ask the janitor or the
corner grocer or her friendly neighborhood child psychologist for advice—but not me.

"After I finished, she said, 'I've listened to your tirade;
now you listen to me.' But I just said, 'I don't have to
listen to you. I don't ever have to listen to you again.'

And you know, maybe that was the first time in the nine years since we'd gotten a divorce that I realized that I really didn't have to listen to her. Maybe she wasn't going to let go of me, but I was going to do my best to let go of her."

Many ex-wives use their children's illnesses—or their own seeming concern about the possibility of illness—as a device for holding on. Worries about a child's possible nervous breakdown are frequently mentioned. One man in New Orleans said that he felt his ex-wife was almost wishing for their daughter to have a breakdown.

"If Janey gets down in the dumps about a test or a boy, I get a call from my ex-wife. Her latest was: 'I think it's better that Janey have a breakdown now, at sixteen, than later on.' It was an accomplished fact in her head that Janey had to have a breakdown.

"I could picture what was going on in her mind. First she'd blame me for divorcing her and leaving Janey. Then we'd both have to consult with doctors, psychiatrists, schools. Of course, that would mean we'd have to spend a lot more time together, something I want to avoid."

In addition to frequent phone calls, there are also the mails. If there are children, there are report cards to be sent, notes from teachers, memos on choices of camp, invitations to piano recitals. And even if there aren't children, ex-wives have been known to send cards and notes on every conceivable kind of anniversary: wedding . . . divorce . . . the day we bought our first boat. . . .

And there are other little memoranda:

"I know how interested you are in collecting old pewter porringers, and I just came across this book, so I thought I'd send it along."

And to complete the idea that ex-wife is watching you, a woman received this short note from her husband's ex-wife: "I understand from mutual friends that Sam gave you a pink wicker-and-glass breakfast tray. I thought you'd want to know that he gave me an identical tray when our son, Randy, was born."

"Legally divorced, but emotionally married" is the best way to describe these wives who won't let go. Very often, the greatest harm they do is to themselves. They remain so involved in what was, that they can't concentrate on what can be.

Of course, should a man decide to marry again, his ex-wife, if she's a woman who won't let go, will double and triple all her efforts to remind them of their life together.

"My wife and I were separated for a year before I spoke to my lawyer about a divorce," said Andrew E., of Columbus, Ohio. "And it was eight months after the divorce became final that I remarried.

"I had no idea how she'd react. When she learned about my second marriage she called me, and screamed into the phone, 'I never would have given you a divorce if I had known you were planning to marry again.'"

Strangely enough, many wives react strongly even if they were the ones to initiate the divorce.

"Get Off Our Back, Lady!"

As one very successful fashion designer says, "My husband's ex-wife actually threw him out of their apartment. She kept the apartment, all their furniture, and he gave her their ski house in Vermont. And even though she has a high-paying job, Bob gave her tremendous alimony, which he is paying today. She said she never wanted to see him again—until I appeared on the scene.

"One night Bob took me to the ballet. His ex-wife, Pat, was there, and she saw me. After that she called Bob daily—in his office and at the hotel where he was living. After we got married, she stepped up the campaign. She decided to move, and she asked Bob over to their old apartment to pick out whatever books he wanted. Then, another time, she asked him to come over to choose some prints. On that last visit she tried to seduce him, the whole tired bit—candles, wine, and the kind of negligee she never wore when they were married.

"I really screamed when I heard that! Bob and Pat have no children, and I told Bob that his ex-wife was playing too great a part in our lives. I mean, she was *there,* the ghost at the wedding feast—that sort of thing. I don't know what Bob would have done—I don't know what he could have done—if Pat hadn't gotten an offer of a great job in Chicago and decided to move there."

Bob and his wife are lucky, because Bob's ex-wife did move, but there is still a viable telephone connection between New York and Chicago, and phone calls kept coming—mostly in the middle of the night. Bob's second wife took matters into her own hands. She made sure to answer the phone when it rang at strange hours, and when she heard Pat's voice, she'd say, "Oh, look who's calling—our little family parasite. Get off our back, lady! Stop wasting all that alimony money on long-distance calls."

Most men who are troubled by previous marital entanglements are not fortunate enough to have a former wife who leaves town. Some divorced men are able to move, and more than a few have asked their companies to transfer them to out-of-state and even out-of-country offices.

But most men don't find it that easy to pull up stakes.

"Maybe if you're in your mid-twenties you can move," a divorced man in his mid-forties said, "but when you get to my age it's not simple to give up a career you've been

building, and start all over again. The most you can hope
for is that your ex-wife will find someone else and concentrate on her own life."

Unfortunately, though, the wife who won't let go per-
petuates her own sad cycle. She works so hard at retain-
ing the semblance of a relationship with her ex-husband
that she puts minimal effort into creating a new life for
herself.

The best thing a man can do for his ex-wife and for
himself, advises one man who is happily remarried, is to
be firm. "Don't let your guilts rule you. Ask yourself,
'Am I really as bad as she makes me think I am?' The
answer will probably be: 'Nobody can be quite that bad.'
Once you can accept yourself as fallible, but not evil,
your ex-spouse has less of a chance of getting to you."

And what about the woman who married the man
whose ex-wife won't let go? It may sound like a children's puzzle, but it's far from a childish game to the
current wife.

The new wife, depending on her own needs and personality, can be kind and do her best to be understanding, or she can get furious from time to time and stamp
her feet in a rage. But whatever she does, or however she
behaves, she will have little long-range effect on the relationship between her husband and his ex-wife. Their
interactions have nothing to do with her.

Many psychiatrists maintain that guilt is the omni-
present force that makes a man believe in the fiction of
a pleasant relationship with an ex-wife who insists on
clinging to their past.

"Stay away from the incurably optimistic," advises
matrimonial lawyer Raoul Lionel Felder. "They ignore
the realities of life and are sure to lead you astray. Don't
trust people who feel all problems can be solved if only
one tries hard enough."

And, adds a Los Angeles divorce lawyer, "Don't believe too much in those so-called civilized divorces. I suppose there are some of them around, but mostly they exist only in Noel Coward plays. If people felt that warmly toward each other, they wouldn't be getting a divorce."

Once a man divorces and remarries, it's important that he doesn't let his ex-wife run (and ruin) his subsequent marriage. If she's the kind who won't let go, she'll try to, employing the triple-threat tactics of guilt, children, and money. She may act out her anger in many ways, doing her best to prove that she is the real wife— the true wife—while the present wife is only the mistress.

Many ex-wives use the telephone to get that point across.

"My ex-wife likes to call in the middle of the night," a man in Denver said, "and she actually asks, 'Is *she* there?' meaning my present wife. For a while I tried to reason with her, and then Beverly had the phone company reinstall our phones on jacks. Now, every night before we go to bed, we disconnect the phones."

"My Daughter Reports Everything"

A Chicago doctor told of bringing his second wife flowers during a weekend when the children of his previous marriage were visiting.

"My daughter reports everything I do to her mother, and after I took the kids home on Sunday night my ex-wife called and said, "How can you give that woman flowers? Especially in front of your own daughter!' I started to explain that my wife is very nice to my kids, goes out of her way to please them. But how can you answer such irrationality?"

An ex-husband has certain responsibilities toward his

previous marriage. If there are children, there's financial support. If there are no children, there may still be alimony, financial settlements, and the need to support an ex-wife—especially if she's an older woman without any work experience.

There are emotional ties to one's children, but once a man is legally divorced it's important that he also become emotionally divorced from his ex-wife. It's easier to do this if a man recognizes that it takes two people to make a marriage, and two people to cause it to break apart.

According to psychiatrists, lawyers, and family counselors, there is no single guilty party in a marriage that failed. Accepting that can make it easier for a man to take two giant steps back from his ex-wife.

Unfortunately, many men find it hard to step away. They act out guilt feelings, and believe that they can't be completely rejecting of an ex-wife. But such concern is more cruel than kind. It may give the ex-wife a feeling of false hope, a mistaken belief that a marriage that has ended has a chance of eventual resurrection.

If a man feels himself to be truly divorced emotionally from his ex-wife, he must express that truth in his behavior. Little get-togethers for dinner or cocktails are not wise. If children are to be discussed, choose a neutral corner—not her apartment or yours, but her office or yours, where there are other people about. The most intimate place a man can safely go to with an ex-wife— if he really feels she is ex—is a coffee shop.

The idea of an ex-wife who still longs for her ex-husband may be soothing to his ego, but the emotional burden that arises from that longing is a large price to pay.

Divorced men should examine their own motives: are they doing anything to imply that they still care or are emotionally involved with their ex-wives? Some men find it very seductive to be wanted in that way.

Sometimes, according to Dr. Levy, if a man has left his wife for another woman, and he knows that his first wife still has strong feelings for him, he can be supportive of her needs, provided his second wife is understanding. "Of course, if the second wife suspects that there are no real problems and what the first wife is doing is trying to win him back, there's going to be trouble. And there are ex-wives who call ex-husbands to solve so-called problems when they would be better off calling a plumber, an accountant, or an auto mechanic—depending on what has gone wrong. Unfortunately, very few couples are civilized when it comes to a divorce."

The best thing for an ex-wife who won't let go is an ex-husband who will. It will free them both, and give them the opportunity to find happiness in a new relationship.

"It's My Fault, Blame It on Me"

HALLIE C.: When Bernie and his ex-wife separated, her parting words were that despite everything, she knew that nobody would ever love her or care for her the way he did. I didn't know him then, but I think it was the kids that kept him there. Ideally, Bernie wants to see the kids every other weekend, but that has evolved after a period of time; originally he wanted to see them every weekend, but I was very insistent about wanting what is healthy for us. And ultimately, I don't think that Bernie really wanted to be with them that much. I didn't say that to him directly; I said, "It's my fault, blame it on me, we're not going to see them every weekend, because I can't stand them every weekend." Meanwhile, he was perfectly relieved; he can blame it on me, but he's perfectly happy.

And his ex-wife was just using the kids to get back at Bernie, so we don't have them exactly every other weekend. It really depends. If we have some other obligation on Saturday, and we don't feel like having them over on a Saturday night, we don't. His ex-wife objects, but she doesn't let it cramp her style. Last week we brought the kids home on a Sunday night and the house was cold and dark and empty; she wasn't there. She does all the typical things—she sends the kids to us in shabby clothes, and she's always telling them she doesn't have any money because Bernie doesn't send her enough, and this is just not true, and she tells this to the kids, and they're very concerned, and they talk about money and say, "We can't afford this," and "We can't afford that."

And yet, though she says Bernie is so mean and cheap, she still tries. Well, one day, it was really a riot. Out of the blue—it had to be eight or ten months since she and I had had any conversation, because when we go pick up the kids, she stays in the house and I stay in the car— but this time she walked out to the car and said, "How are you?" And I think she was helping one of the kids into the back seat, something like that, and she was leaning over and into the car, and her ass was up in Bernie's face, and the two of us were hysterical—we couldn't wait for her to go back into the house. It was really funny—and obvious—that kind of maneuvering.

"I Can Never Be Sure How She's Going to React"

TERESA T.: All the way through, his first wife would— as I suppose first wives do, trying to be difficult—try to use the kids against me, even unconsciously. And I would get angry, and Ives would constantly—seemingly —give in, I mean, give in to the demands of his first wife, because he would say, "I couldn't care less about her demands, all I care about is the children, and it isn't going to help them at all if for some point of honor on your part or my part, they're hurt." And he did the right thing. And now I can handle it, though at first it used to upset me terribly, and she'd still love it if the children hated me, but we have told them to be very considerate of her.

I don't think she'll ever remarry. Whenever she calls, I can never be sure how she's going to react. She called up the other day because she wanted to share the fact with Ives that their younger daughter is taking gymnastics and she's so good at it. But other times when she calls . . . you can't figure it.

"She Was the One Who Wanted Out"

LAURENCE F.: My ex-wife was the one who wanted out of our marriage, but yet she was still the one who made all the demands. She was going to move to New York, and she wanted to put the kids into private school, and at that time there was no money to do all that, and we had to compromise.

Anyway, she wanted out, but she still wanted to run —or I should say ruin—my life. She was out to get me. I was in the printing business and she was working for a publisher who used to give me a lot of work, and she got very catty, and told the people she was working for not to give me any business, even though she was still expecting a lot of money from me. When I think about it now, I remember we were on the phone constantly talking about that, and the kids, and her moving—and everything.

"I Enjoyed Seeing Him With His Children"

NANCY D.: I enjoyed seeing Len with his three children, but what had me terribly upset was when the children all of a sudden came against him. "Daddy doesn't really care. Mommy told us, 'He left the neighborhood, and he's living with some other woman now, and he doesn't give a damn about you.' " And the kids believe this. This upsets Len very much, and I hate to see him hurt this way.

Last week his oldest daughter called up—she's about seventeen, and she's like a mother to the two younger ones—and she told her father, "We're very unhappy with Mom, and we want to come live with you."

But Len doesn't believe this; they've done it before. He feels it's another way for his ex-wife to get back at him. Now that he's cleared up that court business, and he doesn't have to go to court for a while, she won't see him, and there's no way she can do anything to him through the courts, so she yells at the kids, and says things like, "Go live with your father," but it's really like saying, "Go bug your father, call him up, give him a little more grief, say you want to live with him—you know, the way we talked about it."

It's hard; Len said no to them, he said they're going to have to prove to him that they really want to come out here by more than just one phone call. He explained that it's going to be quite a legal hassle to get custody, and if they really want it, they're going to have to fight for it. And we feel that if they mean it, they're going to call back, and we're waiting to see what will happen. This happened once before and we jumped at it. We went ahead and called lawyers, and had papers drawn up, and then Len's ex-wife laughed in his face and said the whole thing was a hoax.

"It's Only a Hundred Miles, But . . ."

LEN D.: That's why I'm glad we live out here. It's only a hundred miles away from my ex-wife, but that hundred miles helps. We find that by being out here, we're very much at peace. We don't get the rotten reminders so often. My ex-wife can always pick up the phone, and okay, we get upset for a few days, but it's at a distance, we don't get involved so much, and there aren't daily reminders. I mean, I don't run into my ex-wife on the street or see her once a week. Also, if she does pick up the phone it's a long-distance call, and she doesn't do that as often as if it were a local call. But you know, with all the hostility, I think to this day she thinks I might come back. I think that's why she's never married this guy she's been living with. And you know, we had a very bitter divorce. There was no other woman, but it was very bitter. I think it was almost the same thing as turning around to a man and saying, "You're not masculine." When a woman loses a man, it's a slap in the face. "How could this happen to me? I'm good-looking. I'm not the brightest, but I'm not the dumbest." The way my ex-wife was taught that marriages work, she was doing all this, having kids and all, doing all the right things—and it didn't work. How could this happen to me? How could my man walk out on me? All these years, she still can't accept it. That's why she still bugs me, why she won't let me go.

"If They Can't Have You, They'll Take Everything Else"

GENE A.: My wife said that if I left her, she'd really get me. She said she'd take everything I had—my home, my business, everything. And she just about did. I left with one broken suitcase and my clothes. Anyway, one Sunday I brought my kids home to her apartment, and when I took them upstairs, I saw one of my books on her bookshelf—just a soft-cover—a pocketbook—you know? Anyway, I took it. I don't remember—I think it was a book on how to play poker. Don't you think she called me? "You took a book," she said. "You better bring that back, it's mine." What can I tell you? If they can't have you, they'll take everything else.

V

The Husband Who Won't Let Go

"My ex-husband still keeps visiting my relatives. He's always asking them questions about me and my second husband."

Carol D., Michigan

"My daughter tells me that when she spends the weekend with her father, he makes nasty cracks about my present husband."

Jeanine C., Texas

"Why is it that whenever my wife's ex-husband comes to pick up their kids, he has to stay and visit with us, and drink all our Scotch?"

George P., California

"My husband says he hates his ex-wife, but he lunches with her about every two weeks. He says it's to give her advice on her investments."

Sonia G., Wisconsin

"You Divorce Me?"

"I still remember what my ex-husband said when I told him that I wanted a divorce," said Madeline G. of

Florida. " 'You divorce me?' And he laughed and laughed, as though he had never heard anything so ridiculous."

Madeline had met her first husband at college, where, she said, "he was the best-looking boy in the senior class." Ten years later, married and the father of two little girls, the "best-looking boy" was still that—a boy —and when Madeline told him that she wanted a divorce, he couldn't believe it. His image was still tied to the picture he had of himself as the campus hero, someone so popular that he could never be rejected.

One man described his wife's departure as "a terrific blow to the ego. It was like having her say to me, 'You're not man enough for me.' " Some men do see their wife's decision to leave them as an attack on their masculinity, while others regard it with the anger another person might feel if he had been cheated in a business deal.

"I gave her everything," said Herman B., a stockbroker in Chicago. "We had a beautiful apartment, a summer place in Wisconsin, and I never said no to her, no matter what she wanted to buy. Charge accounts? She had them all up and down Michigan Avenue. I'll never understand—what more could she want?"

"The husband who won't let go," says Dr. Norman J. Levy, "can be a man who feels he's been treated with contempt. He feels abused. A lot of them say, 'I've been taken,' and they mean monetarily."

Men who feel this way have the need to get even, and should their ex-wives remarry, they're still around, trying to make it as uncomfortable as possible for them. They begrudge any happiness that their ex-wives have found in a new relationship, and they very often use their children to find out what's going on with their ex-wives, or to make their lives difficult.

"When my kids spend a day with my ex-husband,"

said Betty G., "I have a terrible time with them when they come home. They tell me that their father says they could have had all kinds of nice things if I had only stayed married to him. Other times, they report that their father says he sends me lots of money for them, but that he knows my present husband and I spend it on ourselves.

"How can you tell two little girls of four and six that their father is lying? And how can you explain his reasons for telling such terrible stories?"

Both money and possessions are used by husbands who won't let go.

"You'll Never Get It"

"Never believe it if the person you're about to leave says, 'Don't worry, I'll send you that later,' because you'll never get it," said Marta F. "I had a terrible marriage, and I was falling in love with someone else, and I told my husband I wanted out, but he wanted me to stay around, and I wanted to leave. Finally, my husband said, 'Okay if you want to leave, I get all the furniture, I get everything,' and I said, 'Fine, I just want to leave.'

"Well, I did leave everything except my clothes, but I wanted some pewterware that had always been in my own family, and I told that to my husband, and he said, 'All right, you can have that, I'll send it to you.' Well, I spoke to him just last week—we've been apart for three years and we're both remarried—and I asked him for that pewterware, and he said, 'You'll never get it.' "

"How Can You Live Like This?"

Some men try to hold on to ex-wives by giving them things, instead of withholding them. Fran L. left her husband after she discovered that he was having an affair with a next-door neighbor.

"It wasn't just that," she said. "That was just the final thing. We had been unhappy for years. I remember when we were living in California, and he came home from a business trip, right after I opened the front door for him he pulled me down on the floor—right there in the hall —and he practically raped me. Things like that.

"I had been wanting a divorce for years, and Bob had said, 'No, never,' and I was too scared to just up and leave. Anyway, after he started that affair, I had to leave, and then I just wanted to forget him—forget I had ever been married to him. My parents never knew how bad things had been, and they were always bringing his name up, and I didn't want to talk about him.

"I got a little walk-up apartment and a job, and I started buying furniture, and I never wanted anything from Bob—not alimony or a settlement or anything.

"But he kept coming around—and this is after he got married—and he kept saying, 'Let me give you things. How can you live like this? Let me get you some decent furniture.' The big thing with him was that he wanted to buy me a piano—a baby grand, a good one. I had bought myself an old-fashioned upright, and that really bothered him. He kept saying he was going to buy me a good piano and just send it over, and I told him that if he did, I wouldn't let it in the house.

"I just wanted him to leave me alone. I didn't want to see him, I just wanted to forget him—forget our marriage."

Some men can't bear the idea that any woman can forget them—including an ex-wife. They seem to feel that they have left a mark—made an impression— branded a woman, so that other men can only compare unfavorably. The idea of "This woman is mine," very much the way a man says, "This car is mine," is still with us.

How can she have forgotten me? How can she leave me? Certainly their actions, their rage, indicate that these ex-husbands believe their masculinity, their sexuality, has been challenged. And this is as true of men in their late twenties or early thirties as it is of men in their forties, fifties, and sixties. Myths and role-playing die hard, and occasionally a man will act out his rage in an obvious manner.

One woman who divorced, moved to another state, and was living with another man said that her husband would call the emergency fire squad in her city and send them to her apartment in the middle of the night. He would also call her at three and four in the morning.

"And no matter how often I changed my unlisted number," she said, "somehow he managed to find it out."

"I'll Charge You With Being an Unfit Mother"

Some men will go to great lengths to "get even" with the women who left them, and left their egos and self-image highly bruised.

Peter C. was a South African lawyer who had been jailed by the government when his law firm became involved in the defense of members of the African National Congress. After many months in jail, he was freed and he left the country, taking with him his wife, his wife's two children by her previous marriage, who had been legally adopted by Peter, and their little girl.

They moved to London, where Peter became a successful publisher. Both he and his wife understood that Peter could never go back to South Africa without risk of being clapped into jail.

The C.'s seemed to enjoy a happy marriage, and they had another child—a little girl—while in London. But about the time their youngest child was three, Belinda C. fell in love with another man—a South African journalist who had been a close friend of Peter's.

Belinda asked Peter for a divorce, and said that she hoped the whole thing could be arranged in a "civilized" manner. Peter's tone was civil enough, but his message was that he would give Belinda a divorce without any battle provided that she would give him permanent custody of all four children, including Belinda's boys by her first marriage. This Belinda would not willingly do, though Peter did promise that he would send the children to her on all vacations and school holidays.

"If you fight me on this, I'll take you to court," was Peter's ultimatum, "and I won't hesitate to reveal that you're having an affair. I'll charge you with being an unfit mother, and because I'm a lawyer and know how to appeal to a court, I'll get custody of the children anyway—and your name will be smeared all over London."

Belinda protested that she was in no way an unfit mother, and that Peter knew it. Peter agreed, but said he believed the court would look at it another way. Belinda decided to take her chances and fight for custody. The case went to court, and just as Peter had predicted, the court found for him, and he won custody of all four children.

"Peter not only has *our* children," Belinda said, "he has *my* children, too."

How long the two older boys would have stayed with their stepfather is impossible to say, because the story has an unfortunate ending. Peter decided to take a year off from his publishing company to devote his time exclusively to the four children. He even planned to write a book about his experience as both father and mother.

This period in his life was exciting, nerve-racking, and at the same time highly depressing for Peter. He would spend hours speaking of Belinda to friends, while at other times he ran about London with a series of girls, each younger than the one before. Peter's home was always between housekeepers, and finally the two older boys went away to boarding school. In a mercurial flash, Peter sailed his cabin cruiser to Spain, where he decided he would build a house on the coast and raise his children. Later, he sailed back and decided that he would leave the children in English private schools, taking them to Spain only for summers.

Peter now became involved in a multitude of projects, most of which he dropped. Under it all ran the theme of Belinda, and his desire to "show her," to "make her sorry." Peter's frantic behavior came to an end when he suffered a massive heart attack and died. This in no way is meant to sound as though "it served him right," or "he got what was coming to him." Peter was a kind, warm man, but he was in the grip of an obsession that probably contributed greatly to destroying his health and his life.

Sometimes a man may want a divorce, it may have been mainly his decision to leave, yet he still wants the attention, the interest, and the caring of his ex-wife. He will even become extremely jealous should she start seeing other men, though he is already remarried.

Such men seem to have a harem complex. Monogamy is the law in the United States, but through maneuvering with money, these ex-husbands feel that they retain marital rights and control over more than one woman.

A Kansas City lawyer, John D., was able to arrange matters in such a way that his ex-wife remained completely dependent upon him, and though he has remarried, she hasn't. Mr. D. believes he has had a thoroughly amicable divorce.

As he explains it, "My first wife and I have never litigated anything. True, she had to go to court and say that she agreed to our divorce, but there's no court order filed indicating how much I have to pay her, or how much money I have to send her to support our four kids.

"I give her what I can afford to give her, and I rely on her not to cheat me, and to go out and spend only what she thinks should be spent. Of course, she knows I can look into her checking account anytime, but there's no contention between us.

"I have dinner at my first wife's house once a week. The reason for this is that my youngest child is eight and my oldest is seventeen, and there's nothing I can do with children who have such a widespread difference in age, though sometimes I take the older kids to a hockey game and the little girl to something else. But on a regular basis, the best way for me to visit all the children is to eat with them one night a week, and I spend all day Sunday at my ex-wife's house for the same reason. My present wife is agreeable to this."

Both this man's ex-wife and his present wife are feeling the heavy hand of the man who pays the piper. Mr. D.'s first wife is put into the position of cooking dinner for a man who is no longer her husband, and allowing him to preside over her table and her life, as though he were a patriarch straight out of the Old Testament.

"Blackmail," says Dr. Levy. "A divorced man should meet his children outside their home. This confrontation should not be forced upon the ex-wife. He should arrange for a place where the children could meet him, on the front steps, say, or if he comes into the house, she should be allowed to remain upstairs. There's a reason why these two people separated and divorced, and there's no need to play this polite charade, or to make small talk when there's no love lost."

"Warfare Is the Word"

According to matrimonial lawyer Raoul Lionel Felder, the parties involved are truly participating in a charade. "I don't think there is such a thing as an amicable divorce, nor do I think it should, in a psychiatric sense, be amicable. I think it's much healthier that aggressions and hostility come out at this point. If they don't . . . well, I've seen some divorces that were amicable to some degree—never totally amicable—but what happens is that all the real feelings that are repressed come out later in a custody fight, or in running back and forth to modify something. I think it's much better, as the youngsters say, to let it all hang out. You know, get rid of those feelings, get it all out of your system. Every peeve you have, and every bit of fooling around. . . . Let it all come out in the wash, into the open once and for all and then close the books."

"Unfortunately, it's not litigation, really, when people divorce; it's all-too-often matrimonial warfare—warfare is the word."

It may be warfare, but many people have sneaky ways of fighting, and nowhere is this more evident than with ex-husbands who refuse to release their ex-wives—or themselves—emotionally.

An ex-husband's motives for not letting go can be an amalgam of feeling cheated of a possession—he did invest all that money in his ex-wife and their marriage—plus the inability to face a rejection which he feels is mainly sexual. Other men feel attached to an ex-wife by strong feelings of guilt. But there are men who hold on because their egos need the balm of having more than one woman available, more than one woman catering. Some men pay willingly for that attention with high alimony payments or a hefty settlement. Unless a divorced woman is really interested in remarrying her ex-husband, it's a wise idea to beware of the ex who bears gifts. *Soothe me, comfort me, and tell me that I'm quite a guy* is very often the message that an ex-husband who stays, and stays, and stays wants to transmit.

Despite all the stories about difficult ex-husbands, they don't seem to be quite as abundant—or perhaps quite as obvious—as difficult ex-wives. This doesn't mean that they don't exist; but the pattern of a man who is divorced is often different from that of a divorced woman.

According to a number of matrimonial lawyers, some women—not all, but some—respond to the idea of a divorce with a greater degree of toughness than men. One matrimonial lawyer said, "They're more vicious. They'll go further to get what they want than men."

Another, who asked not to be quoted by name—most of his clients are women—said, "Across the board, men are much easier to deal with in a divorce. Women are very difficult to deal with, and when matrimonial lawyers talk among themselves, we attribute this to the fact that for the most part, we are dealing with neurotic, menopausal women. And that's true, because the vast number of divorces we handle are for middle-aged or older people. So we are dealing with people at the point of life where they are menopausal. But we don't really know, of course. We don't take blood samples, analyze estrogen, or anything like that."

(This lawyer was referring only to menopausal women. How do men behave when going through the analogous process? "Male menopause" was not recognized by this lawyer, nor was he willing to admit it existed. However, menopause is a recognized condition in men as well as women, and people often go through hard times when they arrive at this stage in their lives.

Insecurities float uneasily to the surface of the mind; disquieting questions repeat themselves with dreadful monotony: "What have I done with my life?" "Is this all there is?" "Have I missed out on something?" Menopause can affect even good relationships, and it's bound to have an influence on people who are getting a divorce.)

If, as many lawyers assert, women do react with greater anger to a divorce, another reason is that most women have been brought up with the idea that work is a stopgap measure until they get married. Once they get married, they quit work to have a first child, and then stay home to take care of the children and the home. Faced with a divorce, their status (in their eyes) is diminished, their financial security is threatened, and they lash out. Their husbands, as they see it, haven't lived up to the unwritten clauses in their marriage contract.

Statisticians may quote that more women work in America today than ever before, but the figures don't express the feelings behind the dry numbers. More women do work—but most of them do so because they *have to,* and not because they *want to.* The beau ideal is still the good provider, and most women, when they talk of making a "good marriage," still equate "good" with money. The women's liberation movement may change all this—in time. But outside of the large cities, and even within them, many women would agree with the pretty fifteen-year-old girl who said:

"I'd rather be taken care of than liberated."

According to Dr. Levy, women are not more neurotic than men when faced with a divorce.

"Men's neuroses may show in a different way. Men can be more controlled, because that's the way men are taught to be. They tend to *seem* more rational in their demands and expectations; they can always fall back on their work, saying, 'My work is more important, and that's why I spend so much time away from my wife.'

"But if the wife is at home, and is lonely, and her solution is to be loved, she will be more emotional. She will want emotion from the man. She wants the money and the security, but she wants money and security in the setting of the loving experience. She goes crazy when she doesn't get it, and the more she's like that, the more he pulls back; but society excuses his behavior on the grounds that he's busy—he's got to go to the office."

Men seem to cope better, because traditionally they were brought up to be more self-controlled. A rejected man may feel every bit as bad as a rejected woman, but there's still the need to role-play, in accordance with the masculine tradition of self-control, and it's this role-playing that impresses lawyers into believing that men are easier clients than women.

Times, though, are a-changing, and as society allows men to become more open, revealing their true feelings, matrimonial lawyers in the future may well be faced with male clients who act out their rages, and become just as difficult as many women when faced with the prospect of divorce.

Right now, though, what is true for the divorced wife is just as true for the divorced husband. The best thing for an ex-husband who won't let go is an ex-wife who will.

"He Felt I Wasn't Being a Good Domestic"

GINNY V.: My husband—I mean my ex-husband—was the one who wanted the divorce. He fell in love with someone else, and the day after we got divorced, he married her, but yet he tried to keep me under control.

He was supposed to send me a certain amount of money as child support for our three kids, but then he cut down on the money. He felt I wasn't being a good domestic, I wasn't being a good keeper of his children. Of course, his relationship with his children today is zilch—and I did everything in my power to make it continue as a positive thing.

You see, he was angry, because he felt he was paying a full-time housekeeper—that was supposed to be me—and I wasn't there all the time. I had gone back to school, so I was a full-time student with three kids, and he was mad because I wasn't home all the time. He cut down what he was supposed to be giving me to $375 a month, which was not terrible then, but I realized that he was trying to run my life, just as if we were still married.

He was sending me this money, but he was doing all kinds of things that made it impossible for me to have leisure time, and when he made the decision not to send me all the child support, I realized that I had to get out there and roll up my sleeves and go to work and make a life for myself, or he'd be around forever. And who wants a husband who isn't a husband anymore?

"He Was Always Calling My Mother"

ANDREA F.: My ex-husband had never been all that crazy about my family until we got divorced, and then suddenly he kept coming around all the time. He was always calling my mother, and dropping in on my sister and her husband, and he even asked my sister, "How's my family?" meaning *my* family—and he had never given a damn about them anyway.

So finally, one day my sister said, "*Your family* is wondering how come you treated Andrea so meanly. You have plenty of money, and when you and Andrea split up, you didn't want to give her a thing."

Naturally, he said he didn't have very much, though

we all know differently, but he stopped seeing my sister after that.

"My Wife's Ex-Husband Wants to Be My Friend"

GERARD M.: When something is over, it's over, but not with this guy my wife was married to. My wife's ex-husband wants to be my friend—my buddy. We took a place up at the lake this past summer, and guess who came up to spend the weekend with us? Yeah, just like that, why can't we all be friends? Anyway, he showed up with this girl, and it was pretty clear to me that he was showing off in front of my wife. You know, kind of saying, "See, I have no trouble getting girls." I don't know why, but somehow we did let them spend the weekend with us, and it was the damnedest thing. We had people coming over for supper on Saturday night, and he took over—I mean, he acted like he was giving the party. He kept asking people if he could get them something, or make them a drink, stuff like that. Next day we even had to drive him and his girl to the train station. I don't understand my wife. She didn't act as though she minded having him around—though she said she did. And I don't understand myself for letting him stay.

"He Kept Coming Over Every Night"

PHYLLIS N.: When I married Bobby, I had been divorced and I had a son. Well, after ten years I knew that I just couldn't hack it with Bobby anymore, and I told him that I was leaving for the East Coast with Matthew, my son, and that I wanted a divorce. I didn't tell him at the time that I was planning to marry someone else, though I think he guessed.

Well, Bobby made a big speech about how if I didn't want him, he didn't want to be with me, and he only wanted me to be happy. Then he packed his clothes and moved out. Except he didn't stay out. All those weeks before I moved East, he kept coming over almost every night. Once it was to fix Matt's stereo, another time it was because he thought he left some sweaters; always something. And if I had company, he'd just hang around and hang around, and it got so that I'd ask if he wanted to stay to dinner, and he always said yes. I suppose he was just trying to be friendly. no hard feelings, that kind of thing, but for me it was over, and I'm just glad that now we live three thousand miles apart.

VI

Money, Money,
Who's Got the Money?

"The way I feel about it, I'm subsidizing my husband's first wife. What with alimony payments and child support, I'll never be able to stop working. And we'll never be able to afford a child of our own."

Lillian T., Pennsylvania

"Before I got married, I never had any real money problems, and I didn't expect any when I married Janie. But Janie was a widow with two kids. I guess if they were my kids, they would cost as much. But they're not my kids.

Steve M., Ohio

Money and children vie for first position as the biggest problem faced by people who remarry.

Very often the two are intertwined, but even when they aren't, the problem of money is almost always present. *Almost always* because some couples marry after the children of their first marriages are past college age, and their exes are safely tucked into new relationships. In such cases, money doesn't seem to be a problem.

Why does money have to be the thing for most people that goes bump, clatter, and bang in the night? Why do people attribute a life and a personality to money?

"Because," says Dr. Norman J. Levy, "money is power, money is success. It can be my money. Money is possessiveness—and all these things destroy marriages, too. The woman who hides certain amounts of money; the man who doesn't tell his wife anything about what he's earning and doesn't share the financial side of his life, in terms of how much insurance he's got or what provisions he's made—these characteristics reflect something deep in the personality."

If all these money-related factors can cause trouble in a first marriage, they can present even more problems to a remarriage because where there are ex-spouses and children from an earlier marriage, there are more elements to consider. Any number can play—and frequently do. There's my money, your money, our money, your ex-wife's money, my ex-husband's money, my children's money, your children's money, our children's money, and your ex-wife's alimony.

Money can be a weapon wielded by ex-wives and ex-husbands to exercise control or express anger toward people they're no longer married to.

"Some women have a desperate need to be the recipients of money," says New Jersey matrimonial lawyer Paul Silverman. "There are cases we have where the husband's income is maybe a million dollars a year, and I can't ever get those women enough money to make them happy.

"You would think that anything over ten thousand or fifteen thousand dollars a year to support a woman would be a sufficient amount of money if she's going to be happy apart from her husband. But then they start talking about, "Well, I buy my clothes at a couturier's in Paris, and I make two trips a year to Paris, and my wardrobe alone is thirty-five thousand dollars a year. And why shouldn't I be entitled to a new car every two years, and I have to have a full-time, live-in maid, and my house costs me four thousand dollars a month to run,' so even where there appears to be more than enough money, when these people split up there's never enough. So money is always a problem."

This, of course, is true for single people, married people, divorced people, remarried people—just about everyone. Worries about meeting bills, making payments on the car, paying for music lessons or medical care, are certainly not limited to those who remarry. The problem seems more obvious among people who divorce and remarry because there's much loud discourse about who's going to get what, and the specific financial demands and obligations of each person.

The money problem is more acute among people in the middle class than in the millionaire group Paul Silverman was discussing, and why should a woman who had been married to a millionaire be satisfied with ten or fifteen thousand dollars a year in support? It is only fair to consider past life styles—certainly when millions are involved.

People who remarry, and stay remarried, have learned to solve the money problem—or if not to solve it completely, at least they've learned to live with it, often by discussing it openly.

Dr. Laura Singer, a marriage counselor, and a member of a television panel discussing remarriages said, "Some people seem to be embarrassed when talking about money. A lot of things can seem embarrassing, sex can seem embarrassing, but you have to bring these things out into the open."

Some women may be afraid to discuss money matters

with their new husbands because they're wary of seeming greedy and don't want to give a man the impression that they have married him for his money.

Regarding that, Dr. Singer felt, "You don't really rock the boat by discussing things. You rock the boat more by keeping things hidden—and resenting them."

"I'm a Stepwife"

"You know the words *stepmother, stepfather, stepchildren?*" asked Roseanne D. "Well, I've coined a new one —stepwife. That's how I feel. I knew when I married my husband that we'd have to share expenses. He has alimony payments to meet and child support for his two kids, and I make a good living. But sometimes he makes me feel as though his ex-wife is still his real wife, and I'm a stepwife.

"We have a small house in the country. I bought it before we got married, and I still make the mortgage, insurance, and tax payments. My husband does pay if there's some special landscaping to be done, and he also took care of the bills for painting the house.

"Anyway, we go out to our house by train, and we keep an old car at the station. The way we work the financial part of that is that I pay the train fare—which can be high, because we go parlor car one way—and he pays the upkeep on the car.

"Well, one week I got to the train station late and Sandy bought the round-trip tickets. I forgot to pay him for them, but first thing Monday morning he reminded me about those tickets, and I paid him back.

"That part is okay, but the next night he told me that his daughter, Ginny, was starting to see a psychologist, and since Sandy is responsible for both his kids' medical bills, he had immediately sent Paula, his ex-wife, a check for Ginny's initial visit.

" 'And Paula has to go, too,' Sandy said. 'So I also sent a check to cover her session with the therapist.' Too much! In Sandy's separation agreement it says that he'll pay his kids' medical expenses—not his ex-wife's. Besides, Paula has a very good business of her own—she makes more money than Sandy. All I said was, 'Are you going to keep on paying Paula's therapy bills?' And Sandy went kind of green. 'I'm a dummy,' he said. 'She called and asked me for the money for her and Ginny, and I just automatically sent it. That was crazy.' I didn't say anything, because I could see that he felt bad about it. But I couldn't help thinking: Sandy is quick to ask me for money, and just as quick to send money to Paula. He still feels responsible for Paula, still takes care of her, but who takes care of me?"

Sandy, like many men who have divorced and remarried, chose a professional woman who has always supported herself to be his second wife. His first wife didn't start her own business until after she and Sandy had divorced, and he still visualizes her as a woman who has to be cared for. That, plus his continuing feelings of guilt about having walked out of their marriage, contributes to his easy agreement to frequent requests for extra money, above and beyond what is specified in the separation agreement.

Women who have married men who shoulder the burden of child support and/or alimony are frequently irritated by the money they see being sent to another family. They feel resentful about those weekly or monthly checks going to women as payment. Payment for what? For having deigned to marry the man, or perhaps payment for releasing him from an unhappy marriage?

"She Doesn't Do Much but Strum Her Guitar"

Cindy D. has only been married to Sam for one year. She's a social worker and has every intention of continuing in her profession. Sam's ex-wife, a highly educated woman in her early thirties, has no intention of going to work. Her excuse is her three children, all of whom are of school age.

"But why *should* she work when Sam sends her all that money?" asks Cindy. "And this past spring Sam changed jobs. He's not making as much money as before, but still he had to send his three boys to an expensive camp. Listen, in this recession a lot of people didn't send their kids to camp, but camp was in that agreement, and even if we had to borrow money to do it, those kids went to camp. I can tell you that if they had been our kids, they would have stayed home, or maybe gone to day camp. Besides, Sam's ex-wife is home all day. She doesn't do much besides strum her guitar. Why couldn't she have taken care of them?"

Very often the man or woman who wants to be freed from a marriage has to be prepared to pay the price.

"It's like buying yourself out of slavery," said one young woman, recently remarried. "Well, maybe that's too heavy, but it is like being an indentured servant and having to pay your way out. I was the one who wanted the divorce, so my ex-husband decided that he didn't have to give me anything, even though our kids were three and five when I left him. I had to take him to court—for child support, for everything. And I never did get the things that other women I know have gotten—the women whose husbands have left them."

"The Big Problem Was the Dollars"

Because money is such an important element in most people's lives, the sending of alimony and child-support checks takes on a highly personal and emotional character.

"I resented my ex-wife for a long time," said Bruce S. "She was the one who wanted the divorce, and I just wanted to forget her, but I couldn't, because there was a financial involvement. If there had been no money involved, there would have been very little contact between us. I mean, I would have seen my children when I wanted to—I could have picked them up, or they could have come to visit me—but the big problem was the dollars."

The irritating part of Bruce's financial involvement with his ex-wife, alimony payments, ended when she remarried. Bruce never objected to child support, and his two children are about to graduate from Ivy League colleges. Bruce has been happily remarried for almost eight years to Valerie, also divorced with three children. Because he loves Valerie and they're happy together, Bruce is as generous with his money as he is with himself.

"Before I got married, my partner asked me, 'Does Valerie have any money?' And I said, 'You know, I really never asked her.' He said, 'You never asked her? How can you get married and you don't know if she has any money?' So I said, 'She never asked *me* if I had any money. I'm not getting married because of money.' Valerie and I never did discuss it, and we both knew that we'd be able to make it, and money was not the main thing, it wasn't even a consideration. We always knew we'd have a roof over our heads."

"You Won't Have to Support Him"

Like Valerie and Bruce, other remarried people trans-
cend money worries with great generosity of spirit. Will
and Linda D. have been happily remarried for fourteen
years. Will's wife died in childbirth, leaving him with
twin infant boys. Linda was divorced, with one son.
When they remarried, their biggest problem was Linda's
ex-husband, who supported his son, but constantly criti-
cized the way the boy was being brought up, and who
often threatened to leave the country to avoid child support.

"Linda hated seeing her ex-husband," said Will, "she
hated talking to him on the phone. He was more than
unpleasant—he was nasty. So after we were married a
year, and with Linda's okay, I called her ex-husband at
his office. I offered to adopt Linda's son.

" 'You won't have to support him anymore,' I told
him, 'but you won't have any rights as a father either.'

" 'That's fine with me,' was what he said—the bastard.
Anyway, it was what I thought he'd say. I could see he
hated Linda and didn't really love their kid. So we got
together with lawyers, and now Eddie's legally my son.
And I really feel that he's just that—my boy, my son—
so I don't mind supporting him as well as my other two
kids."

"We've Been Getting Orthodontist's Bills"

Most people who remarry are not resentful of money
spent on children of a previous marriage, though they
may feel that the money might be handled more cau-
tiously if the parents had stayed together.

"When my husband divorced his ex-wife, he gave her

everything: their co-op apartment, the furniture, their bank account. He agreed to pay a whopping sum for alimony and child support, and to pay all medical bills, life insurance—his ex-wife is the beneficiary—and education for his kids through college.

"For years now we've been getting orthodontist's bills for Candance, my husband's daughter. Finally, after four years, her teeth are straight. Beautiful! Then all of a sudden, the orthodontist started billing us again. 'What is this?' I asked my husband. 'Does this dentist have you on some kind of automatic billing?'

" 'No,' he said, 'but one of Hank's front teeth overlaps a little, and that's being fixed.'

"Hank is my husband's son, and I've never noticed that one tooth overlaps—and you wouldn't either. And you know what? I bet that if my husband were still married to his ex-wife, and living with those kids, he'd never have that tooth straightened."

"You Have Me"

What most remarried women do resent is the money that seems to go out in an unending stream to ex-wives.

A publishing executive said, "Sometimes I think it's terribly unfair. With what my husband and I make together, we should be rich. I never get a cent of alimony from my ex-husband, but my present husband sends a bundle to his ex. She's got a mink coat and I don't have a mink coat. This really used to bother me a lot, and I would carry on and carry on, but my husband would look at me and say, 'Do you want to be her? Look, you have me,' and you know, he's absolutely right."

"You have me" is a remark frequently made by husbands burdened by payments to their ex-wives that seem to go on forever. "Till death do us part," many of them have discovered, applies not only to marriage but to alimony.

And "You have me" is not as egotistical as it sounds. It is a reaching back to the fundamental idea of "for better or worse," an idea that people who remarry successfully seem to take literally.

Some women regard ex-wives who *don't work* but live on alimony as terrible people; others feel that women who *do work* and accept alimony are the worst. Opinions are based on the personal reality of each particular situation, and the ex-wives referred to are those who are able to work.

Many remarried working women, helping to support husbands who in turn are supporting ex-wives, are confused by the stand they believe NOW, the National Organization of Women, has taken.

"I feel that the man doesn't have a chance at the moment," said the publishing executive. "Women's lib is supposed to change things. I used to think that women's lib would liberate men, too. But it seems to me that NOW is for everything—getting all the rights, and alimony, too. And not just for older women who have never worked—I understand that they can't suddenly go out and make a career—but NOW is for alimony for younger women, too.

"This is so strange to me, because I'm a working woman, and a self-supporting woman, and I've worked all my life, and they're not talking for me."

But according to attorney Raoul Lionel Felder, the women's liberation movement has lightened the burden for some men.

"Women's liberation is a paradox," says Felder. "It's like giving birth to a Frankenstein monster. As a matrimonial lawyer, I've observed that it's hurt women regularly. You don't see these things in the courts anymore

—that a woman is married two years, divorces, and suddenly she gets a million dollars. It doesn't happen anymore.

"The courts start taking into account the woman's ability to work, the length of the marriage, and children, and the bottom line is that she ends up getting less money. It's actually being passed on in some of the statutes, and in cases coming down from higher courts. They call them 'golddigger statutes.' That means someone who's married for a short time, and wants a divorce, and lots of money, won't get it. It's really hurting some women."

"I do more for women's liberation than all the broads I meet, and all the parades the women's lib movement holds. I get women liberated—I get them alimony."

Matrimonial lawyer Paul Silverman agrees with Felder regarding the benefit that the women's movement has had for men. "What you see today that you didn't see ten years ago is that young women who are getting divorced, and who don't have children, are frequently denied alimony, or they get alimony for a very short period of time to tide them over the transition period between being married and being single.

"You no longer see young women without children who are able to sit back and say, 'Well, I'm going to get alimony now for the rest of my life, or until I remarry.'

"And there are some judges, many of them, when they see older women getting a divorce, well, they won't say to the woman, 'You have to go out and work,' because the judge doesn't have that authority, but these judges will cut the alimony low enough so that it's hard for this woman to live, and he feels he's motivating her to go out and get a job, and work, and do something with her life. And maybe that's happening because of women's lib."

If men are treated more understandingly in divorce

cases, why do so many of them end up sending a large part of their earnings to ex-wives? Possibly, as Paul Silverman suggests, because "A person usually gets the kind of divorce that he or she wants." Guilt is often the trigger that makes men agree to "anything, anything." That, and the desire to get out of a bad situation as quickly as possible. The emotional need to retreat quickly from a bad or unhappy marriage comes first, and the actual counting of costs comes later. In much the same way, a woman marrying a divorced man with prior emotional and financial commitments will say, "Don't worry, darling, I'll work, we'll manage—money isn't everything."

And for most people who say that, money really *isn't* everything. But as the years move ahead, they're bound to realize that money isn't just money—it is a weapon, and can be a powerful one.

"That's How I Keep Score"

One divorced woman, an extremely successful financial analyst without children, was asked why she held her ex-husband to his alimony payments of fifteen thousand dollars a year. She had wanted the divorce originally, her ex-husband had given her their apartment as well as their country home, and he had remarried some two years after the divorce, so there had been no "other woman" involved in their splitting up.

"That's right," she agreed, "I don't need the money. But it's the way I keep score."

Often, alimony payments—sometimes large, and sometimes small—will keep a woman from remarrying. One woman without children has been divorced for fifteen years, and has been receiving twenty dollars a week from her ex-husband, since remarried. An attractive woman, who could have remarried, she'd rather have that twenty dollars than a new marriage.

"He'll never forget me, the bastard. Let him think of me each time he writes a check."

Some ex-husbands, who feel that paying out the money is bad enough without actually having the emotionally wearing chore of writing the checks, turn that assignment over to a bank.

A matrimonial lawyer described one case as "the longest non-stop payment of alimony that I've ever seen." The case involved a woman of thirty-two who divorced a man of thirty-four. They had one child, and the man agreed to pay child support until the child was twenty-one and alimony until the woman remarried.

"Well," said the lawyer, "here it is forty years later—she's seventy-two and he's seventy-four. He's been paying alimony all these years. The woman's been living with a guy, but she hasn't married him because she didn't want those payments to stop coming in. The ex-husband inherited a family business, but still—imagine paying money out for forty years to a woman you don't care about!"

"If Two Kids Ate a Total of Eight Meals . . ."

Playing the money game, and keeping score, can be conducted on many levels—some seemingly minuscule.

"My husband's ex-wife is a bookkeeper," said Lenke B., "and she figures everything out just the way she keeps books. She's got a bookkeeping service, and I bet she's good at what she does—I can tell.

"When Alex and I first got married, she rented a house on Fire Island for the summer. His kids would visit us on alternate weekends, and Alex would get an itemized bill for ferry fare, train fare, and taxi fare, round trip.

When they visited us in the city, Alex also had to pay their cab fare to and fro.

"But that's nothing. He was supposed to take his kids to dinner on Wednesday nights, and his ex-wife had that figured out, too. They spent alternate weekends with us, and I'm sure she added all that to her calculations—I mean, how much money she could save if two kids ate a total of eight meals at our house over a period of two weeks.

"You think I'm exaggerating? I know I'm not, because there was hell to pay if Alex missed a Wednesday. If one of the kids was sick on that night, and couldn't go out, Alex had to bring food in.

"I'll never forget the Wednesday night when Alex told his kids that he had a business meeting and wouldn't be taking them to supper. The kids told their mother, and she called our apartment. Alex wasn't home, so I had to cope with her. She screamed at me that she didn't want to prepare an extra supper. Listening to her, I got a sudden chest pain. I mean it—it was like a vise going around my chest. I really thought I was getting a heart attack.

"Finally, when she stopped shouting, I was able to say, 'Look, send the kids out for a hamburger, or whatever they want, and Alex will give you the money back.' That calmed her down."

Scorekeeping is not limited to women or to men, but it does have far-reaching effects that extend into remarriages.

What angers many women is the comparison they can't help making between ex-husbands who pay them no alimony and neglect to pay child support, and present husbands who pay alimony religiously to a seemingly parasitical ex-wife.

"It's the Little Things"

One woman explained that her ex-husband refused to keep up child support for their three kids after their divorce. Rather than endure the seemingly endless hassle of going back and forth to court, she went to work, and developed an important career as a designer.

She still remembers the first years as a working woman. "I got a job for a hundred dollars a week, out of which I paid a young girl—who became like another child—fifty dollars a week. And I got fifty. My ultimate dream was someday to be able to keep the whole hundred."

Ten years after her divorce, she married a man who supports an ex-wife who doesn't work with ten thousand dollars a year in alimony, as well as supporting two college-age daughters. A generous-spirited woman, she commented, "Large sums are not the issue—it's the silly little things. Of course, large sums can become the issue, as when one of my husband's daughters, who goes to school in California, decided to visit us at Christmas time instead of visiting her mother in Mexico.

"My husband is supposed to pay for one trip a year, at Christmas, for his daughters to visit their mother. Okay, but this girl wanted to spend Christmas with us —fine. We loved having her, and my three sons treated her like a queen. So we paid for her trip from California to New York, and back.

"Then came Easter, and she called and said, 'Mommy said I haven't come to see her, and she's so lonely.' So what do you say? We sent her the money for the trip. Another four hundred dollars."

What happens to a second wife, and/or a second family, when money is a question? According to a lawyer employed as a New York City Corporation Counsel assigned to family court, who represents people who come into court without lawyers:

"The second family is entitled to the same treatment, the same protection, that the first family is entitled to. However, a man cannot avoid his responsibility to his first family by taking on new obligations of another family.

"This comes into court all the time, as when a man says, 'I'm supporting my present wife and two or three children, and I can't afford to pay.' The judges take everything into consideration, but they hold that a man does not avoid responsibility to his first family by taking on the new obligations of a second family."

Raoul Lionel Felder confirmed this, and added, "Most states have this law—it's the 'sword and shield theory.' In other words, if a man's ex-wife tries to get more money out of him, he could put up this new marriage of his as a shield to prevent her getting more money, but he can't do this, nor can he use his remarriage as a sword to beat her down and take less money. Now, where there are children from more than one marriage, the law will treat them equally; the children are not going to suffer by this."

One hopes the children don't suffer, but many husbands and wives accompanying their spouses into family court do, when they discover how little status *they* have as compared to ex-wives or ex-husbands.

"This Doesn't Concern You"

Maggie J. was widowed without children for ten years before she married Frank P., a divorced man with two children. Maggie, now the second Mrs. P., worked and contributed her fair share to all household expenses.

After she and Frank had been married for five years, Frank's business took a bad downturn, and Frank discovered that he was borrowing to keep up alimony and child-support payments. He applied to court to lower alimony payments, and the case was heard in family court. Maggie P., before she had married Frank, had purchased a small house in an exclusive resort community. The house remained in her name, and she made all mortgage, insurance, and tax payments on it.

However, during the first hearing in family court, the lawyer representing Mona, the first Mrs. P., got up and said, "How can this man ask to have alimony payments lowered, when he owns a mansion in East Hampton?"

Maggie, who had been waiting outside, was floored when she was told of the lawyer's statement.

"First of all, it's far from a mansion—it's a very tiny cottage. And then, it's mine—I bought it before I married Frank, and I make all the payments on it, and it's in my name. I said, 'Look, Frank, what's Mona's is Mona's, and what's yours is Mona's, but what's mine is mine.'"

At the go-around in family court, Maggie brought all the necessary papers: the deed to the property, the bill of sale, the record of mortgage and tax payments, and canceled checks indicating that she had made all the payments.

She was stunned when her husband's lawyer took the papers from her, but said that she wouldn't be allowed in the hearing room.

"This doesn't concern you," he said.

"It was my money, my house, and it didn't concern me," Maggie said. "I didn't believe him, so I marched up to the door of the hearing room. The guard asked me who I was, and when I told him, he said, 'You're not one of the litigants. This doesn't concern you.'

"I never did get my day in court," said Maggie, "but it was all right, because the judge accepted the fact that the house was mine, and he lowered alimony payments when Frank brought in his IRS records, and showed that his business really was losing money.

"As a matter of fact, the judge went even further—and this part is kind of funny. Frank had agreed to send his kids to camp for one month each—that was all he could afford—but his ex-wife insisted that he should pay for camp for the entire summer.

"Well, she got up and spoke her piece before the judge, about how important camp was, and all, and none of this was appropriate to the hearing, but she wanted it on the record, I guess. Anyway, the way Frank told it to me later, the judge was an elderly man, conservative, middle-class, and of Italian descent. Well, Mona went on about camp—and Frank wasn't fighting it—and the judge raised himself up and said, 'What do you mean, camp? I never went to camp! Kids are better off at home.' Of course, Frank did send them to camp, anyway, but that part was funny."

Do money problems cause a remarriage to end? Yes, if the marriage's foundation was basically financial. There are women who marry richer and older men, but as Dr. Levy says, "If the man wants her to be more than Mrs. Adorable—if he wants her to be Mrs. Productive or Mrs. Share-the-Responsibility—and this wasn't what she bargained for, she'll pull out."

Raoul Lionel Felder confirmed this: "One of the anachronisms of our profession is that we do better in depressions. You wouldn't think so, but money is the glue that holds many of these marriages together. T.S. Eliot had a line—he said, 'We two shall lie wrapped together in a five-percent exchequer bond.' And it's true, you see in these kinds of marriages, if the money's not there, there's no reason to stay married. There are no trips. I mean, if your husband's sitting around, you can't even have your affairs anymore. You can't get away to see your boyfriend, so things are really falling apart."

When people have remarried not because of external or superficial things, but because of a sense of love and relatedness, money—or problems stemming from the lack of it—will not destroy a marriage. As Mildred Newman and Bernard Berkowitz said:

"Isn't it wonderful when two people in a marriage will take care of each other, rather than having it be a one-sided relationship? In some marriages there's one person who is taking care of, and one person who's being cared for, like a parent-child relationship."

Where a deep caring is the force that has created a marriage, that marriage will hold, despite the frets and stresses of money problems. This doesn't mean that people involved in remarriages are so Pollyannaish that they are oblivious to the things money can buy. There may be a few patient Griseldas somewhere about, or some noble men, very old-school-tie, who don't mind handing out money to women they no longer care about—but they're as common as unicorns. Remarried people complain, often loudly; they bitch and they grouse; but if they have something going for them, they stay together.

And a note of interest in these years of the working woman are the many professional women who have no intention of giving up good, going careers, but who express a desire to be "taken care of." And by this they mean financially, though they amend this often secret wish by saying, "Just once," or "Just for a little while." Custom dies hard. Sometimes the attitude remains: "What was good enough for Mother would be good enough for me, if I could get it."

Some people mentioned the number of others who

were depending upon them for support—children, step-children, elderly parents. One woman spoke rather rue-fully about her dependent children and stepchildren, who showed no inclination to search for part-time jobs or to help out partially with their own finances.

It was very different in her day, she seemed to be saying, but if so, that was probably because her parents insisted that she take on gradually increasing financial responsibility. The fault is not in the stars, but rather in the way we bring up our children.

"He Said He Ate in McDonald's"

DEBORAH D. (a lawyer working for the city and attached to family court): I had a case recently, a Florida case, and the father is the typical upper-middle-class well-heeled man, as to the way he lives and the way he conducts himself, and he's paying—well, his rent is over six hundred dollars a month. And his style of living—you know, he goes to the best restaurants. Of course, when I questioned him, I asked him where he ate, and he said he ate in McDonald's.

He actually brought the head of his firm—it's a brokerage firm—and they're on very good terms. He wants the court to believe that he's allowed the use of a Cadillac car for his clients—a car which he admitted he also uses for pleasure, and which he garaged in his building at ninety dollars per month, and on which he paid the garage until recently, and the firm is now paying it. I think it would tax the credulity of anybody that the firm —where he is bringing in practically no business, he says, and his boss testified to that, because he's a friend of his —that this firm would allow him the use of a Cadillac when there's public transportation to almost every place that he would have to go to. Anyway, I tried to bring all that out in the court of examination, because this man has not contributed to his wife's support or the support of his children for many months.

We have many people who come into family court and conceal assets, who hide them in every way in order to deprive their family. Where they're in a personal business, they have ways of not declaring their income on their income tax return. And therefore, people who should not be suspect are often suspect.

"She Hired a New Attorney, and He Wants More Money"

LLOYD J.: My wife wanted a divorce, and I agreed. I even asked for custody of our three boys, but she said no, she wanted to keep them. Anyway, I'm giving her twenty thousand dollars a year—that's both alimony and child support—and everything seemed to be all right, until I remarried. Then I don't know who got after her, maybe some divorced girlfriends, maybe her mother—I don't know—but they said, "Go get this guy." So now she's hired a new attorney and he's raising all kinds of issues about the validity of our divorce—it was in the Dominican Republic, but she had given me power of attorney, which she revoked afterward. They questioned me this past Monday. It was a pretrial hearing held at her lawyer's office—it took all day—and they asked questions I really didn't know the answers to. I think it was a combination of two things—her mother, who had two lousy marriages, and the other, her divorced girlfriends, or the woman that she lives with. Anyway, they asked me—I changed jobs a few months ago—all about the pension fund, and how much was in it, and things like that, and I really didn't know the answers. I mean, I can tell you how much I made in a year, but I can't tell you exactly what was commission, what was pension, things like that. You know what she wants? She wants forty thousand dollars! Listen, I wish I had it to give to her, but I haven't. But I tell you what I wish more—I wish I were a widower.

"It Became an Antitrust Case"

NORA O.: You want to know how we work the money out specifically? Okay, my second husband, George, pays all the bills and my salary buys food, and clothes for my three boys, which are minimal—you know, blue jeans and T-shirts. And when my oldest son took a vacation, we both gave him some money, and I give him an allowance. I spend whatever I earn, and I don't really care.

Now, about college. I have one boy of college age, and two boys who will soon be college age. My ex-husband is paying me now what he should have paid me years ago, because now after ten years without my being vindictive or hostile, George's lawyer discovered that over a period of ten years the sum that he owed me in back alimony and child care was so great that it became an antitrust case, rather than a family court case, and the lawyer subpoenaed my ex-husband and his wife to come to court with all their bills, because what they did when they first got married—which was the day after he and I got divorced—was to transfer all funds to her name, which is against the law. Anyway, it came to over ten thousand dollars, so now he pays me five hundred and ten dollars a month for the boys, and that money will take care of sending the two younger boys to camp this year.

My kids are good about money, they don't ask for what they don't need. They're not savers, but they're not hoarders.

This year, with my one boy in college and my husband's two daughters from his first marriage, we'll have three kids in college. I mean, people say to me, you're married to a successful man, why do you have to work? Why? We have three kids in college, plus George has to pay alimony to his ex-wife. And then we have parents. My generation is caught between long-living, healthy, but dependent parents, and immature, dependent children. We have five kids between us—his and mine—between the ages of fifteen and twenty-one, and they show no signs of independence, and we have three parents, too.

"Ernie Is a Nonearner"

WANDA P.: My first husband was supposed to send me twenty dollars a week for our son, but he usually didn't bother. Sometimes I get a check every five months—whenever he feels like sending it. I sat down, and I realized how much energy, how much money it would cost me to take him to court, so I applied that energy and money to building my own career. I decided I'd come out ahead.

I was very pragmatic. You've got to look at the cash value—how much energy will it cost you to hate him for not sending the checks on time? I spent that energy on a second job.

Anyway, when I got married the second time, to Ernie, I said, "Don't worry, I'll support my son—you don't have to worry." So money wasn't a problem with us at the beginning, but it's become that since. At the beginning, Ernie's business was new, and basically I would say that Ernie is a nonearner. He earned enough to take him skiing, and this and that, but he had no tremendous drive. Through the years I think Ernie has leaned on me too much, because I'm the strength there as far as money goes. And we don't like to spend money the same way.

Ernie is sports-oriented, and I'm aesthetically oriented, and it makes for a difference. Ernie can go out and spend two hundred and fifty dollars on skis, where I can go out and spend two hundred and fifty dollars on a table. I have more aesthetic values, I like decorative things: clothing, beautiful dinner parties.

Ernie thinks he's very protective of me. I mean, he goes bananas if another guy touches me or admires me. I guess he's protecting me, but that's not the kind of protection I need. The kind of protection I need is a few thousand dollars in the bank. A little bit of knowledge that if I broke my leg he'd be there. My whole thing is a monetary thing, and a lack of confidence in Ernie to support me, or support us. We have terrible money problems, even though we don't have a lack of money.

"It's a Mixture of a Curse and a Blessing"

DORIS W.: I have always been self-supporting—in my first marriage, and now in my second—and sometimes I resent it. I think it's a mixture of a curse and a blessing. It's a blessing because I am by nature very independent and I don't want to lean on anyone for money; yet I resent it, because so many women have financial advantages and they don't have to do a thing. They don't even have to be beautiful, or a good lay. And I feel it's a bit of a curse on me that my being independent financially has been an advantage to the men, rather than to me.

Though I do resent it sometimes, I try not to show my resentment too much. Philosophically, I don't like to equate money with human relations—you give so much, I give so much. I think the two should not be equated.

There are contradictions within me. I would like once—once—to be showered with financial support, either as a wife or as a mistress. I don't care how. I would like that feeling once. I've never had that luxury. And I'm very financially insecure—that's my greatest insecurity. I have no one to depend on if I get old or infirm. So I have a tremendous fear of that—it's my one really great insecurity. Listen, marriage is never marvelous. I have a reasonably happy marriage, but there is no such thing as anything being total. I tell you, though, if I got married again, I would only marry for money. I would not marry again unless there was an equitable financial arrangement.

But, you see, the problem is that I don't need a man for money, and that's why marriage may be difficult to my husband, but just once I'd like the security of knowing that the money is coming from somewhere else—not from my own resources.

"They Throw These Figures at You"

EMMETT J.: When my first wife and I got divorced, the judge—the lawyers—they throw these figures at you that are accepted as the norm. "One-third of your salary is definitely going for support, and this, and that, and the other thing. And that's the way it is." I fought that. I said, "Why does it have to be this way?" And you know how it worked out? It worked out that at the beginning, I was sending my ex-wife and kids 75 percent of my salary. I was sending her a hundred and twenty dollars a week. And then when I couldn't send my ex-wife all that, she'd have the satisfaction of hauling me back into court—getting me under the gun.

The court structure at the moment is definitely for the care of the children. This means that by using the children, the woman very often has the guy so wrapped up, so twisted, that very often he'll quit a good job, or he'll stay at one level, because every time he gets a raise, more money goes right back out to his past.

I very seriously thought of leaving the state, but I think it would have destroyed me. I don't think I could have handled complete solitude. I didn't want to be alone —with strange people—and that fear kept me from moving to a new spot, and starting all over.

Well, when I got married again, June and I moved away. It's not too far, but it's far enough; it helps. And then I decided to go back to school. I'm in my mid-thirties, but I'm back in school—how about that? But I couldn't do it without June. She's the main support—financially, every which way. I get part-time jobs, of course, but June's the one working full-time. It's a two-year course I'm taking, but every few months I have to go back into the city, to family court, to prove that I'm not working full-time, that I am going to school. Because of that, they did lower child support.

"There's Always Going to Be Something That You Can't Do"

JUNE J.: I sometimes think that if Emmett's three kids were here, we wouldn't have to send the alimony and the child support, so we'd have some extra money here. Granted, it wouldn't be easier, but if you make spaghetti for two, you may as well make it for five. I could learn to cut back a little more as far as food is concerned, and I was thinking—hoping—that Emmett's family could help us until Emmett is out of school. I'm sure they'd be willing to help financially, because it's for the kids—you know, the grandchildren.

I think that's the biggest problem when you marry

someone who's been married before. You have to accept the fact that there's always going to be something that you'd like to have, or like to do, and that you can't do, because you're constantly sending money to the other family.

"I Have Problems With Asking People for Money"

BOBBIE T.: I have a fantastic job that affords me an enormous amount of freedom and flexibility, and I am my own boss moneywise. I have problems with asking people for money. I did with my father, I do with Don. It's not Don's problem, it's mine. My therapist and I spent some time on this. I feel as though I can do what I damn well please—which does not mean that I do— if I earn my own money, and when I can count on myself, and when I don't have to report to anybody.

I earn a big salary, and I can do what I like in my own house. If I didn't make any money, my sole justification for existence would be that I was running the household for Don, and I would feel guilt-ridden, I know myself. This is very important to me.

Anyway, Don has all this alimony and child support to send to his ex-wife, but the only time he and I exchange money is when occasionally Don leaves money for the cleaning woman if I don't have cash to leave her. I can't tell you what it takes on my part to ask him for a few dollars.

The way we work it is, Don pays the rent and I pay everything else. It probably comes out pretty even. I'm not a clothes horse, so I don't have many problems about that. Most department store things I buy are gifts for other people. When Don buys clothes on a charge, and the bill comes in, if I don't have the cash to cover it, I say, "Don, your bill at Marshall Field's is something I can't handle, so here it is." I don't feel bad about that.

But otherwise, I pay everything. If he's bought a couple of turtlenecks on sale, and it's twenty-five dollars, I don't think about it. But if he's bought two suits, and it's five hundred dollars, I say, "I'm sorry, I can't afford it, you have to pay for it." I'm not going into my savings for that.

And he has a checking account and I have a checking account; I absolutely refuse a joint account, and that raised a big discussion. One of the fights that we had—we would go to his ex-wife's house to pick up the kids, and Don would disappear and come out half an hour later. He was balancing her checkbook, because she had never in her whole life done it.

"She Kept Making Me Desserts With Whipped Cream"

DERO V.: When I left my first wife, I left with nothing, just my clothes. I moved into Gina's apartment—we weren't married then—and I think if it hadn't been for her, I wouldn't have eaten. I mean, I had my business, but it wasn't so great, and I gave a lot of money in alimony and child support. Anyway, at that time Gina paid the rent and the food. And I was lucky in another way—she's a great cook, and kept making me desserts with whipped cream, which was a very soothing experience, especially at that time. I'm not kidding.

Anyway, eventually I got divorced, and Gina and I got married. Gina works, and I still pay child support, though I have gotten the alimony reduced. I also pay all medical bills, dental bills, camp bills for my kids. Plus I keep an insurance policy with them as beneficiary, and I'm responsible for their college—and that's only a year off for my daughter.

Gina pays the rent, I pay the food, the laundry, and the cleaning woman. We share vacation expenses. We bought an old car, and we each paid half. Gina is a big present-buyer, and I pay most dinner checks—except every now and then it's on Gina. She buys her own clothes and pays her own medical and dental bills. I think everything is pretty fifty-fifty. Gina bought a new air conditioner, and I'm having the bathroom redone. What can I tell you? Sure, we have money problems, but they're not with each other. It's just that we'd like to have more. But who wouldn't?

VII

My Brother The Lawyer

"When I split up with my first wife, I went to my brother the lawyer for help. He didn't approve of what I was doing, so he drew up a separation agreement where I promised to pay for everything. I'm still paying, but I'm not talking to my brother any more."

Gordon D., New York

"One of the elements that make up the $215 in court costs in a Philadelphia divorce is a $15 fee that every divorce applicant has to give to the Philadelphia Bar Association . . . what does the money go for? To maintain the Bar Association's midtown luncheon club in the Adelphi Hotel."

Murray Teigh Bloom, *The Trouble with Lawyers* (Simon & Schuster, 1968)

Unless you're widowed, a remarriage is preceded by a divorce. And according to many people who go through the process, their divorce might have progressed with greater ease if they could have handled all the details without benefit of lawyers.

Why this great disaffection with lawyers? Why do so many divorced people agree with Shakespeare's "The first thing we do, let's kill all the lawyers"?

Of the people interviewed, many changed lawyers during divorce proceedings, while others felt that their lawyers did not do their very best for them, and still others said, "I wish I had had my ex-wife's [ex-husband's] lawyer." Some happy few felt that their lawyers handled their cases with dispatch and a true feeling for the needs of their clients, but the people who felt affirmatively about their lawyers were in the minority.

"Just Because You're Sleeping With This Woman . . ."

Some of the complaints stemmed from choosing what was obviously the wrong lawyer for the particular case. When Gordon D. decided to get a divorce, he went to his brother, a successful practitioner of general law.

"I'm too close to the case," Gordon D.'s brother said. "I feel too emotionally bound up in the whole matter. So I'll hand the matter over to my partner and good friend, Phil. He'll advise you. But don't worry, Gordon, I'll be there at every meeting you have with Phil."

One sunny Saturday morning, Gordon went to his brother's office to consult with Phil; true to his promise, his brother was there through the whole event.

The first thing Phil did was to try and dissuade Gordon from seeking a divorce.

"You've been married for ten years, and you have two children," he said to Gordon. "Can't you and Faith work things out?"

Gordon explained that he and Faith had had an unhappy marriage for many years, and that he had fallen in love with another woman, whom he wanted to marry. This was no news to Phil, who had been told that by Gordon's brother.

"Look," Phil said, "just because you've been sleeping

with this woman, it doesn't mean that you have to marry her."

Gordon said it wasn't a question of *have to,* but of *want to.* Phil then suggested that rather than start immediate action for a divorce, Gordon initially apply for a separation.

"You can see later on how you feel."

Gordon, guilt-ridden about his children and his wife, and made to feel still more so by Phil and by his own brother, agreed. Phil drew up a separation agreement, in which Gordon agreed to the following: He had recently put a down payment on a cooperative apartment, and according to the terms of the agreement, he would continue paying for the apartment, and deed it over to his ex-wife. He would take out a large life insurance policy and name his wife as beneficiary, so that if something happened, his children would be provided for. He would give his wife all the money in their savings and checking accounts; he would pay all outstanding department-store bills; he would pay all medical, dental, and camp bills for his children; he would give his wife and his children money for support that came to approximately 75 percent of his income.

Gordon did make some small protest about the amount of money, but Phil reassured him.

"Don't worry," the lawyer said. "If you ever do decide to go for a divorce, we can renegotiate the terms. What you agree to give now won't have anything to do with the final decision on alimony or child support. Just sign this; it's without prejudice."

Gordon signed the terms and Phil said that he would call Gordon's wife and then her lawyer, who had been a friend of the D.'s, to tell him the terms.

Gordon left the lawyer's office feeling not as though he had been taken, but as though he had committed mur-

der. His brother had been at the meeting and had said
nothing, but his silence and Phil's comments had made
him feel guiltier than ever.

Later that day, Gordon saw the woman he was planning to marry, and told her of the terms of the agreement. She said, "Maybe it would have been better if you
had gone ahead for the divorce."

Gordon said, "I've done enough damage for one day."
Sufficient unto the day is the evil thereof.

Shortly after that, Gordon went to a psychiatrist, and
began what was to become a two-year course of therapy.
As the weeks went by, he began to realize that he was
not an evil man, that it takes two to make or break a
marriage, and that he was entitled to look for happiness
elsewhere.

Gordon decided that he wanted to go ahead and get
a divorce, but remembering Phil's lectures, he decided to
seek another lawyer. He found another attorney and
brought him a copy of the separation agreement.

The lawyer agreed to handle the divorce, but advised
Gordon that he'd probably have to continue making all
the payments specified in the separation agreement.

"But I was told it was without prejudice," said Gordon.

"Why should your wife take less now?" the lawyer
asked. "You've already given her everything, and now
you're the one who wants the divorce. The time to make
deals is before you sign an agreement, not after. You don't
have any bargaining power left; you've given it all away."

Gordon discovered that indeed he had given it all
away, and he would have to give still more if he was to
get his divorce. By now, a year had passed since that initial meeting in his brother's office, and one day his brother called to say that he, too, was planning to get a divorce.

"And I've learned a lot from what happened to you,"

he said. "I'm giving her sixty dollars a week, for both alimony and child support, and nothing else. If she doesn't like it, let her take me to court."

"If that's the way you're handling your divorce," said Gordon, "why didn't you advise me to do the same? How could you have sat there and let me sign everything away?"

"Well, at that time," his brother admitted, "I didn't think you should get a divorce, and neither did Phil. We didn't approve of what you were doing to Faith and the kids, and we figured if we made it real tough on you— took all your money away—we'd force you into going back to her. I'm sorry, Gordon, I guess I was wrong, but you've got to understand—I had to think of my niece and my nephew first."

It was an expensive lesson for Gordon to learn that it's best not to consult your brother, even if he is a lawyer, when it comes to divorce.

"I thought my brother's loyalties would be a hundred percent with me," said Gordon, "but I was wrong."

Whether you choose as your lawyer a relative or a complete stranger, it's a good idea to leave quickly if he starts making moral judgments about your life and the way you plan to live it. A lawyer is a trained technician, and it is hoped that he can lead you as easily and safely as possible through the legal maze that often surrounds divorce. He is not meant to be a father confessor or a psychiatrist, however. A good lawyer does not try to impose his own values on his clients, and an ethical attorney will not take a case if he feels that it goes greatly against the grain of his own beliefs. It would have been better for Gordon if both his brother and his brother's partner had told him at the beginning that they didn't want to handle his case because they didn't approve of his actions. By arranging for Gordon to sign a separation agreement that was so burdensome to him, they didn't act in good faith as lawyers representing a client.

"If anything," says Gordon, "they represented my ex-wife, and I'm still paying heavily because my brother and Phil felt that they had the right to make moral judgments about my life."

Not all brothers who are lawyers would behave as Gordon's brother did, but it is surprising how self-righteous family members can behave when they're called in to handle a divorce within the family, or asked for counsel on post-divorce matters.

"I Get Nothing"

"My second husband's uncle is a lawyer," said Nelly J., "and you should see the will he drew up for my husband's estate. I'm not even named as a co-executor in the will. My husband's uncle would be in complete charge should my husband die. And then, the uncle has it so arranged that all life insurance policies have my husband's children as beneficiaries, with their mother as trustee. I get nothing, even though I've lent my husband money to go into business. Some of this is my husband's fault, sure, but a lot of it is his uncle's; he's so busy protecting the interests of my husband's ex-wife that he doesn't think of me as a wife. I guess this is because my husband and his ex have two kids, and we have no children together."

"I Played Mr. Good Guy"

One attorney, who is a fellow of the American Academy of Matrimonial Lawyers and limits his practice to matrimonial law, objects to one of the canons of ethics that lawyers are supposed to subscribe to.

"One of the canons of professional ethics," he says, "requires lawyers to expend a wholehearted effort toward effecting a reconciliation before they undertake matrimonial litigation.

"Well, I fly right in the face of that particular canon, because I don't think that by virtue of training, or any other thing, I have the particular ability to play God, and to intercede in someone's life.

"As soon as I become convinced that a client is not acting impulsively, or out of anger, and the client says to me, 'I want a divorce,' I make absolutely no attempt at reconciliation, because behavioral science is not something in which I have any training or facility.

"I had an experience that made me feel very strongly about this. I had a client years ago, and I did what the canon of professional ethics said I ought to do. I talked to this client about effectuating a reconciliation. At the point she came to me, she had a fairly new marriage that she was convinced wouldn't work, and I reached out and got hold of her husband. We had some kind of meeting, and I played Mr. Good Guy, and I was spouting, 'Why don't you kiss and make up, and live happily ever after?' I guess I was persuasive, because that's what they did. They kissed and made up, and left my office. And that was the end of the case.

"Except that about a year and a half later, the same woman was back to see me again, wanting a divorce, but this time she had a ten-month-old child.

"Now, whatever the underlying problem was in their case, I had no ability to analyze, isolate, or determine what it was. So I sent them home to try again, and then when the divorce went through there were three people involved instead of two. If I had done what this woman wanted me to do the first time around, she would have been a reasonably young woman unencumbered by a child. She could have gone out to face the world again and it would have been much easier to find another mate. And her husband would have had no particular financial burdens. Second time around, I had to represent a woman who was encumbered by an infant, and her husband now had to face the prospect of paying alimony and child support for the foreseeable future.

"That's why I think that canon of professional ethics which says that the area of reconciliation has to be explored, and we have to spend effort on it, is an anachronism. Lawyers have no training in how to cope with this kind of problem, and to just tell people to kiss and make up doesn't begin to scratch the surface of what's wrong in their relationship, or what's motivating one or both of them to seek a divorce."

Another attorney, Raoul Lionel Felder also feels that a lawyer can't set a bad marriage to rights. Most often, neither can the principals involved. "You can't knock a bent nail into the wall straight. If you're married to a man who's an alcoholic—well, get rid of him, forget it. People can't reform other people. Psychiatry is terrific, if you've got eight years to spend on somebody, but nobody's worth eight years of time from day one.

"If I were a woman, and self-supporting to any degree and married to an average wage-earner, I would try to get support for my children and forget about everything else. Chances are you'll get more support, because the money is meant only for the children, and child support has to be maintained legally. A man will pay child support, but for many men, to pay alimony—they feel as though they're feeding a dead horse. I mean, there's no reason for a man to keep doing this—no emotional reason."

"We Decided to Tell the Truth"

If a lawyer knows enough not to play God or psychiatrist in a divorce case, what else can go wrong to make some clients feel that he has not done right by them?

"It was all so debilitating," Stephanie A. said, "the whole legal system and both our lawyers. My second husband pays his ex-wife an awful lot of money, and I suppose we could go back to court to see about getting it reduced, except that I couldn't bear that whole legal hassle again. Going to court is terrible, we both went through a lot, and I lost a lot of respect for the judicial system, even though my father is a judge.

"You see, my second husband and I made a decision that I discovered later on was wrong—we decided that we would tell the truth. His ex-wife's lawyer decided that they would lie, and I kept on saying, "We'll win because we're telling the truth,' and they won because they lied.

"We changed lawyers, but it wasn't any help. Our lawyer didn't seem to be on our side. The year before my husband got his divorce, he was working on commission, making a tremendous amount of money, which he and his ex-wife spent on marvelous living, which is fine. But the year he went for the divorce he had a different job, and wasn't making so much, but they looked at the other time, when he was making lots—so what he pays now to his ex is all out of whack. And you'd think our high-priced lawyers could have done something about that, but they didn't.

"Would you like to know what our two divorces cost us? They cost us a total of twenty-five thousand dollars, and I left my ex-husband everything, and my present husband is giving his wife everything. It's not fair."

There are many reasons why remarried people who have gone through a divorce feel that their lawyers were not always fair. Some of the unfairness can be traced to political involvement.

"My lawyer was a friend of both of ours," said Julia D., "and that was a mistake. I was living with my ex-husband in Florida, and this lawyer was politically involved in Florida. He was planning to run for political office, and the family I was divorcing from were Floridians. Their business was down there, their vote was down there, their support was down there.

"He wasn't my ex-husband's lawyer, but still I don't think he gave his all. I think he allowed me to take the least amount of money—twenty dollars a week for my son, who was just two years old then. And then, while the divorce proceedings were going on, my little boy became terribly ill—he had a blastoma—and my lawyer didn't do anything about getting me more money, or medical expenses for the baby, or anything. Now, this was twelve years ago, and he didn't charge me a great deal—he only charged four hundred and fifty dollars—but he didn't fight for me either."

What happens when one of the people getting a divorce is a lawyer? Denise V. says, "My ex-husband is a lawyer, and he bluffed me and I believed him. He even attacked me physically, but I didn't call the police; I didn't want the shame. He was an attorney, and respected, and I protected him even then. I still put him on a pedestal, and that was a mistake. He talked me into giving our son into his mother's care, and he said he would prove all kinds of things about me if I didn't.

"I had a lawyer, but he just did what I asked him to do. I collected no alimony—my ex-husband didn't have any to give at that time. I made no demands about money, but I do feel that my lawyer felt closer to my husband—you know, the brotherhood of the legal profession, things like that."

Fortunately, not everyone who has dealt with a lawyer

feels that his trust has been abused. Some people feel that it is "the system" more than lawyers that's to blame.

"I had a very good lawyer," one divorced and remarried woman said, "and the sum my ex-husband agreed to give me was phenomenal, but each time I was supposed to get it I had to take my ex-husband to court. That's the system, and the wheels of justice grind slow. I won every case, but I had to be the one to reinforce the laws, by going to county court each time."

"Get a Killer"

What to look for when hiring a divorce lawyer? Knowledgeable people who have been through divorce advise others to get a "tough" lawyer.

"Get a killer," says Gordon D. today. "Don't be like me—a gentleman. A friend of mine who's in the midst of a divorce right now—he could say a lot of things about his wife, but he says he still wants to be a gentleman. That's fine, except that she's no lady, and she'll kill him in court. I just hope his lawyer is a killer, too."

Are there lawyers who are "killers"?

Yes, says Kirby A. "The first lawyer I spoke to I wasn't happy with; then I had lunch with a friend who was getting a divorce, and he was using this law firm, and I knew some of the people there, so I switched.

"They assigned me this young guy, and we had certain differences of opinion on how to do things and behave, and this lawyer said, 'Why don't you move back in? That would make it tough on your wife, because she's the one that wants this divorce, but she's making all the demands for money, and until this is settled you have every right to live in your own house.'

"Well, I thought, What a bastard! and I wouldn't do that because it would be destructive to my kids. But you know, my wife changed lawyers, too, and she went to one of the top divorce lawyers, and then I was glad I had my own killer lawyer. I was glad I had this tough guy on my side, because if you don't, you have a lot of problems resolving the situation. It all comes down to who's going to get what. The money, the estate; how much you're going to give the kids and how much you're going to give for alimony."

Kirby's second wife, who was also married before, feels that her lawyer was extremely capable, though he was far from being a "killer." "I'm extremely satisfied with what my lawyer did for me," she said. "But my divorce from my first husband was not a bitter kind of thing. I happened to know my ex-husband's lawyer, and he was a friend, and he wouldn't even take the case until he knew it was all right with me. My own lawyer was also a friend, and it was no hassle."

"Things You Never Learned in Law School"

What do lawyers say about matrimonial clients, and the divorce laws in the United States? Raoul Lionel Felder gives a course that's attended by his fellow lawyers on "The Practical Aspects of Matrimonial Cases." Felder says he lectures on "things you never learned in law school. One of the things I teach lawyers is how to practice defensive law. Doctors have been doing this for years, you know, practicing defensive medicine."

Felder practices defensive law by getting clients to sign memos indicating that they have read the divorce and/or separation agreements at least twice, and that they understand all aspects. He also tries to halt any dispute with a client the minute it arises, doing his best to nip it in the bud, and he tries to turn away certain would-be clients.

"You have to recognize the danger signals," said Felder. "Any adverse personality characteristic you notice at the beginning in a client will be magnified as time goes by. As soon as you start seeing that, you know you have to stop certain things. A client can be questioning you in a particular way, and if he looks suspicious, you know that suspicion can potentially grow like a cancer.

"There are two ways you can be questioned—the questions can denote two things. *Why* from a legal viewpoint, or *why* from a psychological motivation. The first *why* is proper, the second is not.

"First they'll ask, 'Why are you doing this?' and the next thing you hear is, 'My husband is paying you to do that.' This is a very common kind of fantasy among women getting a divorce.

"Now, the men have their own fantasies. The men's fantasies are that the woman's lawyer and her psychiatrist are sleeping with her. That's the men's fantasies.

"The woman's fantasies are that her husband is paying me off, that he's having her followed, that the phones are tapped, that he can fix the judge. And the universal fantasy both men and women share is that each one is getting the short end of the stick."

And why do so many clients end up hating their lawyers after the divorce? Why do they feel they have been badly or unfairly used?

According to Felder, "The thing is that everyone who walks into court is terrorized at the last minute. I would say that twice a month, at least, some woman will come in here and say, 'I never wanted to agree to that, the judge forced me, and my lawyers forced me to settle, and I want to take it back.' And this is very hard to do, because the law is very strict about rescinding agreements made on trial in court.

"What really happens is that you're put into this tremendous pressure cooker, and you're encouraged to make a settlement. People make a decision, and then they think they've made a bad decision. Part of their decision was based on the terrible pressure they're under, but their spouse was under the same pressure.

"And this is one area of law where you are subjected to, or you're a victim of, the judge's marital state, whether he had a fight with his wife in the morning, his religion. . . . All these are factors that shouldn't play a role, but they can't help but do so. The judge can't check his humanity at the doorsteps of the court."

Felder believes that because of the highly unusual and emotional problems surrounding matrimonial cases, all early hearings should be held before a three-judge court. "In the mix," says Felder, "you'd be guaranteed a certain uniformity."

According to Felder, the reason that so many matrimonial lawyers have adverse things to say about women clients is that most women seeking a divorce will see a lawyer who specializes in matrimonial law, while men often go to the lawyers who handle their regular business. Is there a point in seeing a specialist? Felder, who does specialize, is quick to say:

"I don't believe in the specialist business. I believe that there should be a distinction between lawyers who go to court and lawyers who don't. That's important, I think. I think any lawyer who's astute can master any matrimonial case if he has the time. The key phrase there is 'if he has the time.' There are a lot of victims in matrimonial cases, because there are a lot of emotional nuances, and if a lawyer doesn't have the time, the only thing he can substitute is expertise and insight.

"If he doesn't have either experience or insight, he's not going to do a good job. What I suggest to people with limited means is that they go to their family lawyer. I suggest that they go to somebody they can call at ten at night. He may not be the most expert guy in the world, but he will take the time to look it up in the lawbooks."

Felder also suggests that someone on the verge of divorce should not agree to pay or accept a temporary sum of money, even though that sum is accepted, supposedly, "without prejudice."

"There's nothing without prejudice," said Felder, "not in this world. For example, legally the term 'without prejudice' can mean that a woman has accepted a temporary amount of a hundred dollars a week, but that this has nothing to do with what she'll get at time of trial or final hearing.

"However, the fact is that you're dealing with human beings. The judge is a human being, and I've never met such a perfect instrument of justice that we can just isolate some people from their psyches. If the judge sees that a woman has taken voluntarily, and without prejudice, one hundred dollars for the past eighty-five weeks, I'd like to see him award her less than ninety-five dollars, or more than one hundred and five.

"Because we can't get that practicality out of his mind —the fact that she has managed on that hundred dollars a week for all those past weeks."

Felder also recommends that, once divorced and remarried, people should try not to keep on rehashing the details of their divorce. "Nobody walks away happy; everybody thinks they haven't made the best deal. With women, particularly, there's a certain syndrome. If a woman talks about her divorce to her best friend, that best friend has got to give her the little knife, twisting it somewhere to make her feel that something was not right, or that she got taken advantage of, or whatever.

"I don't think men are like that, but maybe I just don't know, or maybe I don't have time for these conversations. But what I tell a woman is that if you talk about your divorce with another woman, one of you is going to go away feeling lousy, and you stand a fifty-fifty chance of it being you, so why get involved in the discussion?"

"Get It Written Down"

SUSANNE W.: One thing I learned after my first marriage and divorce was to get everything written down. I got this idea from all the papers flashed back and forth when I got my divorce, and there were all those lawyers referring to bills, and agreements, and such.

Now, in my second marriage—it's my husband's second marriage, too—we have a written contract. It's a signed document, and it states everything: about my job, and that I plan to keep traveling, that we're not going to have children, how often we have to see his family and mine, how the money is going to be handled. Even who does the dishes.

I've read some studies that say that marriage is great for men, but not so great for women, because married women have a higher rate of mental illness than unmarried women, take more drugs, and have a higher suicide rate. That's because up to now, women had to pay a high price, to make all the adjustments, when they got married, and then they got beaten down when they got divorced—I know I did. Well, I now say get it all written down. If something does happen, you'll stand a better chance.

"My Wife's Lawyer Was One of the Best"

MAC J.: My wife's lawyer was one of the best; he was written up in *The New York Times*. But I feel as though

I beat both lawyers—hers and mine—because I couldn't keep my mouth shut in court.

I was actually brought up on contempt. Her lawyer started out by saying that he wanted me to pay $2,500 for his fee, and I had just read this article in the paper, and he had said in it that people in my class—common people—he wouldn't charge more than $500. And I had this paper with me, and I just read it to him, and I said, "I'm really surprised. It says here that you treat the average Joe—which is me—for $500."

And I said, "Here's the article from *The New York Times*. It says that he's always helping everybody, and is really into his clients. And I'm the average guy, so why can't I give him just $500?"

And you know what happened? The judge just looked at him and said, "The man is right," and they reduced the fee to $750. Well, the lawyer demanded the fee right then and there, and the judge said, "Over a year's period."

What got me is that I had shown my lawyer that article in the *Times* beforehand, and I had said, "Look, this guy is a real hot-shot," and he said, "Oh, don't worry about it," and then when her lawyer introduced that $2,500 fee, my lawyer said nothing.

"All of a Sudden, When a Guy Wants a Divorce, He Finds He's Got a Partner"

RAOUL LIONEL FELDER: The divorce law is protecting women more and more, because there's more and more of a trend toward equitable distribution of property in the marriage. One of the problems we have in America is that we don't have a national law of divorce and marriage. It's a creature of the state. The incongruity is heightened in a megalopolis like New York because you have people who are New Yorkers one hundred percent, except that they commute every day from Greenwich, Connecticut. Their business is here, their friends are here, they have grown up in New York. All of a sudden, when the most personal thing in their lives happens, namely divorce, they're trapped in an alien set of laws, and they have to go to alien lawyers, and they're bound by principles in their personal lives that don't bind their corporate lives, and things like that strike close to home.

New Jersey has a law that people there like to call community property. It's not community property. What the law says is that the judge may divide the property of the marriage as equity may allow.

So you have a case where a man has built up a nice business, right? And he has a little nest egg, and he's in his fifties, and a New Yorker. But he wants to let his kids, who are now teen-agers, get a little more air, so he moves to Fort Lee, New Jersey, and it takes him less time to get to his office than it did when he was living in Brooklyn. Wonderful!

But all of a sudden, if this guy wants a divorce, he finds he's got a partner. It's equitable distribution, and his wife can now take half his life savings. That works in the reverse, too; you know, there are a lot of women with money, too. We need some kind of national divorce law.

VIII

Where Did All My Friends Go? And Why Isn't My Mother Talking to Me?

"When my wife and I split up, she got custody of the house, the car, the kids, and our friends."

Garry M., Illinois

"I was a widow for three years before I remarried. A lot of my old friends dropped me. Now that I'm married again, they're coming around. Now I'm not so sure I want to bother with them."

Karen O., Massachusetts

"One thing about my family: the moment I decided to divorce my wife, they rallied solidly—behind her."

John L., Philadelphia

One thing you can count on in a second marriage: you're going to lose old, dear friends and make new ones. If you're divorced, you'll find that friends take sides, some supporting you, others your ex-mate. Often friends drift away, feeling that they're faced with a choice they don't wish to make.

"A good buddy of mine said that he'd have to stop seeing me, because his wife is my ex-wife's best friend," a man married for the second time said. "He said his wife would kill him if he stayed friendly with me and my second wife."

"Always Room for an Extra Man"

Widows tend to be dropped more quickly by their friends than widowers.

"It seems there's always room at the dinner table for an extra man," one woman said, "but I've heard plenty of hostesses say that an extra woman spoils a table— makes it seem unbalanced."

Widows, when they remarry, are often welcome once again in their old circle of friends. Some women are happy to reenter that particular social scene, while others, resenting the treatment they received before their remarriage, choose to make new friends or to accept their husband's friends as their own.

Divorce, followed by remarriage, often has a strange effect on the couples who are friends of the divorced pair. One divorce among a group of people often sets off a chain reaction, and other divorces follow.

"My good buddy got a divorce," David S. said, "and about a year later, so did I, and then another friend of ours did, too. I guess the first guy showed us that we didn't have to settle—we didn't have to be unhappy for the rest of our lives. Would I have gotten a divorce if he hadn't gotten a divorce first? Maybe—eventually. But I'm not positive."

"They Had Grown Up Together"

Often friends feel that they have the right to be judgmental about a friend's behavior. As Marian J. said, "Webb probably lost more friends than I did when he got a divorce, because he and his first wife grew up in the same neighborhood together, and a lot of their friends were friends to both of them—they had all grown up together. And when there's a divorce, some people think the wife is right, and some people think the husband is right. Some of Webb's friends sided with his ex-wife more than they did with him, but I wouldn't consider them good friends any longer."

"I think another reason my friends dropped me," added Webb, "is that my divorce made their wives nervous. Maybe they figured that if I could leave my wife, their husbands could leave theirs."

"I really was surprised the way practically all my friends dropped me, while my friends' wives stayed loyal to my ex-wife," said Garry M. "I came to the conclusion that most of my friends were people I had met through my wife. I was working, and she was meeting women in the building—women in the park where she took the kids —women in the Parent-Teachers Association. Then she'd invite these women and their husbands over for dinner, and that's how I got to meet the men. I suppose you could say that we were friends through marriage, and when the marriage broke up, so did the friendships."

"Even My Dentist Got Into the Act"

Many people are surprised to discover that everyone feels entitled to comment on a remarriage. Men, despite popular legend, love to gossip every bit as much as women are supposed to.

"Even my dentist felt he had the right to get into the act when I got a divorce and married again," said Nick W. "I've known Greg for years, but he never socialized with me and my ex-wife. Anyway, I got divorced and remarried, and he already was divorced, and later got married again. My second wife and I spent some time with him and his second wife, and I thought he was my friend, until my wife recommended a friend of hers to him as a patient.

"You know what Greg told her? He said, 'I think Nick is still in love with his ex-wife; he wouldn't complain about her so much if he still didn't have some deep feeling for her.' Amateur psychologists! I wish he had stuck to fixing teeth.

"On top of that, my ex-wife started taking my kids to Greg, so then he had to tell my wife's friend that he thinks my ex-wife is really very nice, and every bit as good-looking as my second wife. Okay, that's plain silly, and it doesn't matter. But who is he to sit around comparing my two wives? And to my present wife's friend yet! What a dummy!

"He knew that my ex-wife and I were having a lot of troubles about money. And one day I told him I had to postpone an appointment because my wife and I were going to Mexico. 'Mexico,' he said. 'If you can afford to go to Mexico, why can't you give Roberta the money she's asking for?' The money Roberta wanted was for some dental work she had had done—not by Greg— about three years after our divorce.

"It was Greg who originally advised me not to pay it, because he said it had nothing to do with any dental work Roberta had done while we were married. Now, all of a sudden, he was giving me a lecture, and it was 'poor Roberta.' He's a damn good dentist, but I'm going to look for another one."

"My Friends Were Surprised"

Sometimes friends seem to melt away because life styles change, and proximities become altered.

"My friends were surprised when my wife decided she

wanted a divorce," said Bob R., "and then I moved back to the city from the suburbs, and I was separated from the people I had seen every day. A few of them kept in touch, but for the most part, I made a new life, or picked up old friends whom I hadn't seen in many years. It's the same way with my present wife—she doesn't really see too many of the people she had been friendly with when she was married the first time. I find that people are put in a very difficult position."

Many people who are happily remarried, and deeply involved with each other, feel that the very nature of friendship changes, or comes to be regarded by them in a different light. A first marriage may be based on highly superficial reasons, but a good remarriage is created of far different clay, by people who have arrived at a more complex set of values. Those values also apply to the new set of people who may become friends.

As Barton D. said, "When you get married the second time, you find that one of the important things is to be able to accept a way of life that's your own, and not to hang it on everybody else's life. To be able to do your thing, and not to worry if you're not in line with everybody else. In my first marriage, the social thing—sociability—was a very important thing, to me, and certainly to my first wife. We had all these people around us that we really thought of as good friends.

"Now, in my second marriage, I don't mean we don't have friends—you can't move away from relationships and into a shell—but my wife and I are most important to each other. Neither of us has this great drive to be something to everyone. We see fewer people on the outside than I did when I was married the first time, and neither of us feels uptight about what we do, or the way we live, or whether we go out every Saturday night.

"When I was married the first time I was in my early

twenties, and I know I was a very conventional, conservative person. I'm much less conservative now that I'm in my fifties. I'm much more relaxed now. A lot of that is from having been divorced. That changed me. I became much more independent, and I realized I could function as an individual—I didn't depend on other people's approval. When I was married the first time, my friends' opinions of me seemed a lot more important than they do now."

Many people who divorce are surprised when their friends react with approval.

"My friends were gleeful," said Steffi S., "because they thought—even though they didn't tell me until after—that my ex-husband treated me badly. They were very critical observers of Jim's attitude toward me; they could see that he was always putting me down. Anyway, when I say 'gleeful,' I don't mean 'Ha ha, serves him right'; I just mean that they were very supportive of me.

"One couple managed to stay friends with both me and Jim. They love us both, and we're all friends to this day. I also still have a relationship with my ex-husband, because he and my present husband like each other very much.

"I decided that because I had a child, I had to swallow a lot. I had to go to Jim's house and spend time with my son. There was a period when that was the only way I could see my child or be with him."

"She Is the Mother of Tom's Children"

Friendships, defecting or loyal, are not the only relations that may become strained when people marry again. There's a large network of family to consider: one's own family, ex-in-laws, and new in-laws. Parents who are also grandparents are very often the most difficult when faced with their children's divorce.

"It isn't that I don't like Tom's new wife," one woman said, "but I can't help feeling loyal to his first wife. After all, she is the mother of Tom's children, and she's got custody of them, too. If I don't want to lose touch with my grandchildren, I feel I just have to be nice to their mother."

That line—"the mother of his children"—has haunted many a woman in a remarriage, especially if there are no children of that remarriage.

"I actually ended a friendship with some people I had known a long time," said Winnie J., "when my friend Mira started defending my husband's ex-wife. Mira knew what a hard time she was giving my husband, but she actually said, 'After all, Winnie, she is the mother of his children,' as though that excused every rotten thing that woman was doing. She did say later that she hadn't meant it the way it sounded. But how do you suppose I felt? Especially since my husband and I don't have any children."

"Don't Be Mad at Us"

Sometimes if friends really have taken sides after a divorce, the result can be tantamount to open warfare.

"I'll never forget the first year Maury and I got married," said Mary P. "His children were spending Thanksgiving with us—our first Thanksgiving together —and I decided to make a really big event of it by inviting Maury's entire family for Thanksgiving dinner.

"When the kids arrived the day before, Maury's daughter, Tina, told me that Hope, her mother, had gone away for the holiday, but that good friends of Hope's from Boston would be using her mother's apartment while they were in town. I knew that these people—

Candy and Terry—had been friends of Maury's, too, but that had broken up when he married me.

"Anyway, shortly after the kids walked in, the phone rang, and it was Candy. She introduced herself, and sounded perfectly nice and friendly, and said how much she and Terry would like to see Tina and her brother, George.

" 'I wonder if we could pick them up tomorrow,' she said, 'and bring them back to the apartment for a short visit.'

"I explained that I was planning a big Thanksgiving dinner, and that Maury's entire family was invited, and that they were expected at one o'clock.

" 'Oh, we won't keep them long,' Candy assured me. 'We could come for them about ten and bring them back at twelve—plenty of time before Maury's family arrives. And you know we don't get down from Boston very often, and we'd so love to see Tina and George.'

"Well, she sounded nice enough, and I really believed that she wanted to see Tina and George, so I said okay. The next morning she and her husband drove up, and the doorman buzzed, and I sent the kids down. I figured that Candy was being diplomatic by not coming up. I told Tina that I was expecting her and George to be back by twelve, because the family was coming at one, and I was planning to start serving at one-thirty or so. I wasn't really too concerned about the time because I had explained everything to Candy.

"I went ahead and finished cooking this huge Thanksgiving feast, and set the table, and put extra hangers in the hall closet. Twelve o'clock came and twelve o'clock went, but the kids still weren't back. I tried calling them —they were supposed to be with Candy and Terry at their mother's apartment—but there was no answer.

"Maury was furious. He *had* said he didn't think that

letting the kids go off that way was such a good idea, but I was still trying to be Goody Two-Shoes at that point, and I had persuaded him.

"One o'clock and still no kids, and Maury's family are prompt, and they all arrived between one and one-fifteen. You have to know Maury's family to understand this, but believe me, they're crazy about all the kids in the family. That's all they seem to care about—the kids. When Maury got divorced they gave him a very hard time, because of what they thought he was doing to the kids.

"Anyway, there they all were, and no Tina and no George. And every person who had walked in had said after a very brief hello, 'Where are the kids?' So I had to explain to my brand-new-in-laws—all nineteen of them —just what had happened. Meanwhile, Maury was getting madder and madder, and we kept calling and calling, and I kept taking the turkey out of the oven and putting the turkey back in the oven, and still no Tina or George.

"Finally, at three o'clock, by which time everyone was in a lousy mood because they were starving, I got Candy on the phone.

" 'Where are the kids?' " I asked.

" 'Why, we took them out for Thanksgiving dinner,' she said, sweet as pie. 'I thought you understood that.'

"Well, I started to yell and scream, and there was Maury's family, all gathered around, listening to me carry on, and finally I told Candy to get those kids home to us at once. Twenty minutes later they arrived by cab, and when I opened the front door to them, Maury's family was right behind me, waiting to greet them.

"Before I could say a word, Tina started to talk in a weepy-quavery voice. 'Don't be mad at us, Mary, please don't be mad. Candy said if you have to be mad at anyone, be mad at her.' What a performance! I just knew that Maury's entire family must be thinking that I was some kind of monster who probably beat the kids up. I couldn't help it, I burst into tears. That was one of the worst days I ever had in my second marriage, but when I calmed down I realized it had taught me something— not to trust old friends, who might, like these, take sides, and not to try and please everybody."

Can't fight 'em? Don't join them—ignore them.

"What's Going to Happen to the Kids?"

If people seem more critical during a divorce if they are grandparents as well as parents, they are often even less supportive of a son than of a daughter. The reason is simply that children are usually in custody of the mother, and parent-grandparents are afraid of losing touch with their grandchildren.

"My whole family was terribly supportive of Amy, my ex-wife, when we divorced," said John L. "All I kept hearing was 'What's going to happen to the kids, why don't you think of the kids?' Finally, I said to my mother, 'Don't you care if I'm happy, Mom? I'm your son.' And she said, 'That's always been your problem— all you care about is having a good time.'

"But it wasn't just my mother. I remember one holiday when my sister invited me for dinner and asked me to bring my kids. I told her that I couldn't make it, and she said, 'Then I hope you don't mind if I invite Amy.'

"What got me about that was that my family had never really liked Amy during all the years we were married, but the moment I decided to get a divorce, they changed. I could have understood it if there had been some kind of warm relationship there that my sister had wanted to continue. Besides, everybody knew that Amy was giving me a very rough time over the divorce.

"So I said, 'It's your house, and I can't tell you who to invite. But if you invite Amy, just don't ever invite me again, that's all!'"

A markedly different attitude was displayed by Beatrice N.'s parents when she and her first husband divorced.

"My mother cut my ex-husband's face out of every photograph in the entire album," she said. "And she didn't talk to my ex-mother-in-law, who had been her friend for a long time, until I told my mother, 'If you don't talk to her, I'm going to throw you out of my house. It's not her fault.' And you know, I could never convince my mother—or my ex-mother-in-law—that I was as wrong as my ex-husband.

"I want you to know I'm still friendly with my ex-husband's mother. She loves to come to visit me and her grandchildren. She was very supportive of me when her son and I split up, and as a result, my second husband now has two mothers-in-law, because my first husband's mother also spends the holidays with us."

"It Was No Tragedy"

Families and friends represent fewer problems when a remarriage takes place between two people who were widowed. Except, of course, where there's money involved.

One aggressive forty-three-year-old businessman mentioned at a dinner party that his mother had recently died. He brushed away the polite condolences with, "Look, she died in her sleep at seventy-two. She had a good life, and a good death. It was no tragedy."

"Except to her," one of the other dinner guests murmured, but the high-powered businessman ignored that, and went on to explain that his father was living in Florida, managing the company's branch office in Miami.

Ten months later this son suddenly decided that he missed his mother more than he had expected to. His father had taken up with a comely widow in her sixties, and the son was now very worried about what might eventually happen to the family business. A business started by the father, who still held the lion's share of the stock.

The son and his older brother flew down to Florida and persuaded their father to spend a fishing weekend with them in the Florida Keys. Once away from the pretty widow, the father agreed to sell his sons his share of the business, the share that they would have inherited if their father hadn't planned to marry again.

"It cost us," the son said, "but now it's ours. After all, if my father marries again, he could leave part of the business to her, to her kids, or to her grandchildren. This way we're sure."

"They Said All the Right Things"

Occasionally, people who remarry can't help wondering: What do his or her old friends think of me? Do they like me more, less, or as much as that ex-spouse?

"My husband and I went away for a weekend with a couple who had been friends with my husband and his ex-wife," said Marty T., "and I couldn't resist asking, 'Do you think you could have done this with Olivia and Wally? Do you think you would have had as good a time?"

"Of course, they said all the right things, but I really believe them, because we still see a lot of them, and we always have a good time together. That's not true of all of Wally's friends. He had two other friends, and they were very close; all three of them married their high school sweethearts. Anyway, I liked one of the other couples very much, and the guy was very involved with Wally, but since we've gotten married we've only seen them twice.

"I understand them, but Wally seems somewhat hurt by it, though I think he understands. They must have decided at the very beginning that they didn't want to divide themselves. They were friends of both Olivia's and Wally's, and they walked the tightrope as long as they could, and then it got to the point with us when they just couldn't. They haven't maintained extremely close relationships with Olivia, but their kids are friendly with Olivia and Wally's kids, and they live in the same suburb, so that's where it's at."

Another man, in much the same position as Wally, received a different response from two of his close friends when he told him that he and his wife were divorcing.

"Good," he still remembers his friends saying. "We're not surprised. Just remember—we want custody of you."

"What Kind of a Girl Is That?"

While many people do receive warmth and support from family and friends when they divorce and remarry, others report that it sometimes takes families a longer time to adjust to the new spouse and the new situation.

Marco V. said that his family disliked his second wife, Donna, intensely at the beginning, and remained loyal to his ex-wife for a long time.

"You see," he said, "at first Donna and I were living together, and my parents couldn't see that. They said what kind of a girl is that, who'd live with a man before being married, and take him away from his children?

They felt I should stay with my children, no matter what. My kids are their only grandchildren. They felt I should make do with my ex-wife no matter what. Now, though, they see that my ex-wife is a miserable woman, and they dislike her intensely, and as far as they're concerned, the best thing that ever happened to me is Donna."

Donna feels that Marco's parents started changing when she and Marco got married.

"They came to the wedding, and Marco's father said, 'Best of luck, and I'm glad you got married—finally.' "

"You have to realize," said Marco, "that our backgrounds were ethnic. An old Italian family on my side, and an old Irish family on my ex-wife's side, and both our families are Catholic. The older people really came down on me. My mother asked, 'How can you do this to God?'

"But I wasn't thinking of God or religion, I was just so fed up I couldn't take it anymore. It was a sin to watch what my family went through. They felt I was breaking up the whole family system, and then how could I tell my parents that my children were really using them? Kids are very calculating, they're beautiful little machines, and you have to give them credit for being able to do their manipulating at such an early age. I used to watch them get five dollars out of one grandparent and ten dollars out of another. They'd walk around on weekends with more money than I had.

"But that all ended very sadly when my ex-wife decided that my kids couldn't go visit my parents, and she told the kids that they weren't to take anything from their grandparents. Sometimes my parents will drive over to their house and try to give one of the kids a birthday present or money, but they've been told not to take it, and if they do take it, they get smacked around.

"My ex-wife is very vindictive, and when you remarry, I think more of the burden—the problems are on your second wife. There's Donna; she married me because she wanted me—just me, that's all. But I came with a lot of things—my children, my ex-wife, my ex-wife's family, my family, all set in their minds about my being married twelve years to one woman, and then here comes Donna. I told Donna before we got married that I hoped she was prepared for the past that would come back and haunt us."

"There's Never Been a Divorce in My Family"

While Marco's family took a while to accept Donna, Edwina F.'s parents were quick to offer love and acceptance when she told them that she was planning to divorce and subsequently remarry.

"This was a very interesting thing," Edwina said, "it's a wild thing. One of the reasons I stayed married for fifteen years is that I was under the impression that my parents would be very unhappy. There's never been a divorce in our family. That's what my parents always said.

"When I realized that I was falling in love with Perry, I called my parents and said, 'I'm getting a divorce, and I'm falling in love with another man, and I can't stay this way and be married.' And my father said, 'My God, that's marvelous; we always hated Edmund.' And I said, 'Why didn't you tell me?' And he said. 'We're not the kind of parents who interfere.' And now they're wildly in love with Perry.

"And another thing. My parents are very religious, conservative people, and they used to tell me that if I married someone who wasn't Jewish, they would hold a burial service for me—that's the very old religious way.

And Perry isn't Jewish, and yet they love him so much —I don't think there's anybody but their children they love so much.

"It's funny, because I called and first I hit them with the divorce, and then the fact that Perry isn't Jewish, and over all, the important thing was that they wanted me to be happy. Another funny thing. My father came to see me and he said, 'I have to talk to you about something very important before you get married.' He took me to lunch—I remember it was a Chinese restaurant—and he said not a thing, and then I realized that he had it all planned, not to say anything until the end.

"And finally, what he said was: 'I know that Perry isn't really religious, and he doesn't practice anything. Do you think he would mind converting to be a Jew, and then he wouldn't have to practice that?'

"I said no, Perry wouldn't do that, but it was all right anyway—my parents really love him."

"The Reaction of a Lot of Men I Know Was What Surprised Me"

KENNETH Y.: My wife and I had been married for ten years when I decided to leave her and get a divorce. Yes, there was another woman, but she was no femme fatale —and no kid either. She was someone who wanted to give me the love and the warmth I had never gotten during my marriage.

The reaction of a lot of the men I know was what surprised me. One of my closest friends, Jim, took me to lunch day after day, trying to talk me out of it. He was married, with kids, too, and he'd been a big swordsman during most of his marriage. I knew that—everybody knew it, I guess, except his wife. Anyway, his argument was that I shouldn't leave my wife and kids, but should continue having affairs, the way he did. I had had affairs all through my first marriage; it started right after I was married. I kept telling Jim that I was in love and wanted more, and Jim kept saying I was crazy. He had one idea he thought was just great. He wanted to organize a small party, where he and I and some of our friends would all get together with our mistresses for dinner. I don't know why—maybe he wanted to compare them. No, it didn't come off. Anyway, Jim wasn't the only one. A lot of the men I know aren't happily married and play around a lot. They all kept telling me that I shouldn't do it, shouldn't get a divorce, that I should stay put.

Well, that was almost eight years ago, and my second wife and I are really happy together. The funny thing is that after we got married, Jim broke up with a girl he'd been having an affair with for years, and he seems to stay closer to home, or if he doesn't, he doesn't talk so much about it. He's also crazy about my second wife, and now he says it was the smartest thing I ever did in my life.

Would you believe that there are guys who have stayed married who still ask me a lot of questions about me and my second wife, and whether we're really happy?

I had drinks just the other night with a guy I know is miserable with his wife, and when you're with them you can see she's just as unhappy. Well, he was giving me a hard time, asking me if I really don't cheat, and if not, why not, and telling me in detail what a great time he has with all his extracurricular lays. It got to be pretty bad. He was actually putting me down for not making it with other women, so finally I just said, "Ray, you really hate your wife, don't you?"

And he went bananas! "What makes you say that? Why shouldn't I love my wife? She's blond, and pretty, and smart. Why shouldn't I love her?"

"I don't know," I said. "Why shouldn't you?"

It's strange, because another thing happened later the same week. I was having lunch with another guy I see from time to time, and he's no trash-mouth like Ray, and he was very serious when he asked me, "Are you still happy with your second wife?"

I told him that I was. I think what gets these guys is that maybe, secretly, they were hoping I'd fall on my face the second time, too, because I did something they didn't have the guts to do. I wasn't willing to settle.

"My Second Husband Had These Really Good Friends"

NICOLE L.: My second husband had these really good friends, Max and Caroline. He and Max had been friends for years, long before Max had married Caroline, and I guess that Lorin considered Max his best friend. He told me before we got married that they probably wouldn't remain his friends, because Caroline is very close to Lorin's ex-wife, Emily. I told Lorin that maybe Caroline would react that way, but that Max would always be his friend.

They live in San Francisco, and they called to say they were coming to Boston and would like to get together with us. I had met Max once before; he had come to Boston for a medical convention before Lorin and I were married, and he made a point of looking me up. He had asked me a million questions. He wanted to know about my first husband—I'm a widow—and about my work, and where I was brought up, and where I went to school, and he even asked me for a photograph. I gave him one. I was sure he was going to take it home and show it to Caroline.

When they arrived in Boston, they went right over to Emily's apartment—they were staying with her. They

left their son there and then they came over to our apartment in Brookline. The moment they were inside, Caroline rushed over to the living-room phone to call Emily
to tell her that she was *here.* After that she hugged and
kissed Lorin, and told him how much she had missed
him. She followed him out into the hall, where we keep
our bar, and I could hear her say, "Oh, Lorin, you know
how I love Emily, and you know how I've always felt
about the two of you. At first I couldn't stand it—I hated
you. And I couldn't understand why Max was so loyal
to you."

She went on that way a bit longer, and then they came
back and we had our drinks. A little while later, Caroline
asked me where the bathroom was, and I got up to show
her, and you know what she did? We have a big, old-
fashioned apartment—lots of halls, and doors, and closets—and even though I led the way, Caroline opened
every door we passed—closets, cabinets, doors to rooms.
I figured she was going to give Emily a pretty detailed
description of everything in my apartment.

I finally got her to the bathroom, and after that she
made some calls on the bedroom phone, and later, when
we all went in there to get our coats, she was on the
phone, calmly reading some mail I had left on the telephone table. She was reading a letter, and talking, and
she didn't finish the letter until she had gone through
both sides.

That was a long evening. We went to dinner, and then
we came back for brandies, and Caroline and Lorin were
in the hall again while he fixed drinks, and after, Lorin
showed Caroline some of the books I had illustrated, and
I could hear her all the way to the living room:

"But do you really love her, Lorin? I mean, really? Or
is it just that you admire her talent—maybe that's all it
is."

No, we haven't seen them since. Oh, once we ran into Caroline in Jamaica, and I did my best not to talk to her, and Lorin and Max sometimes exchange a letter, or Max calls Lorin if he gets into Boston for a convention or something like that. I'm sorry Lorin and Max aren't friends anymore—I mean, for their sake. But what I'm really sorry about is that I was so damn civilized with Caroline that night at my house. Now I'd know better.

"My Family Rallied Around"

AUDREY K.: I was in my late twenties when I got married, and my husband had an ex-wife and three children. Everybody always asks: Didn't your parents try and talk you out of it? But my parents—my whole family—were super. My mother treats my husband's three kids as though they were her very own grandchildren. And my two sisters, when they give a barbecue, or any kind of party where their kids are going to be, always include my husband's kids—really make them feel like an important part of the family. Yes, there are problems, but not with my family—and not with my husband's family either. His mother told him after he got divorced that she had always hated his ex-wife. Isn't that something? And she's terrific to me.

"I May Not Be Invited Back"

LUCY D.: We gave this dinner party one night, and it turned out that almost everyone there was either divorced, remarried, or about to be remarried—except my friend Claudine, who's never been married.

Before she left that night, she looked at everybody and said, "I think I'd better run out and get married, and divorced, and remarried—or I may not be invited back."

"His Wife Threw a Knife at Him"

STAN J.: I have a very good friend who lives in California, the home of community property. He didn't put me down for getting a divorce and remarrying, but he said he could never do it. He has all kinds of very serious moral reasons, like he'd feel guilty about his wife, and what about his daughter, and his parents would be upset, and so on.

But I know the real reason is the community property law. He's loaded, but he wouldn't want to give up half of what he's got to his wife. Meanwhile, he told me a story that he and his wife had a big brannigan in the kitchen of their big, expensive house. It was while she was slicing bread, and she threw the bread knife at him.

Yeah, she really did that, and it was a lucky thing he moved fast and ducked. She cried afterward and said she was sorry. But imagine living with a woman who feels murderously about you. It looks like his money is worth more to him than his life. It's like that old Jack Benny joke—you know, where he gets held up, and the guy says, "Your money or your life," and Benny says, "I'm thinking, I'm thinking."

IX

Sex Rears Its Lovely
Tousled Head

"During my first marriage, I was an unsure guy. My wife blamed me for everything that went wrong—and that was in and out of bed. I thought that's the way all marriages were. I'm married again, and I have a great relationship with my wife—in all ways. I used to play around a lot the first time I was married. Now my straying is confined to just staring."

Mike P., California

"My first husband was no fun, not sexually or any other way. It was 'Wham, bam, thank you, ma'am.' Besides that, he made me feel that I was the one who was no good in bed. I'm having a wonderful time with my second husband, and he's made me see that there's nothing wrong with me."

Elspeth G., Florida

"Love is lovelier the second time around," according to songwriter Sammy Cahn, and that's fine, but what about sex? According to people who are happily remarried—and for some, that happiness may not have been achieved until the third or possibly even the fourth time around

—sex definitely is lovelier in a good remarriage.

There was an old-fashioned idea encouraged by certain medieval poets that it was possible to separate love into two categories: the courtly and the profane. Some twentieth-century swingers have adopted that idea and claimed it as their own, insisting that it's possible to have a super-marvelous time in bed with someone without feeling a single deep emotion. But honest people, unafraid of being accused of marching to the sound of a different drummer, say that it's just not so. Sex is better if you feel something about the other person—and it's infinitely better if that feeling is love.

"Look, how good can you be with a guy in bed," said Elena L., "if you hate his guts? Or let's say you don't hate him, but you don't really like him too much. That's how I felt about my first two husbands. Sure, I pretended, a woman can do that, but that wasn't much good for me. I really feel sorry for the guys. They can't pretend—they've got to get it up. It's so different now that I'm happily married. Neither of us has to put on any kind of act."

Which comes first when a marriage breaks up—sexual problems, or problems of communication and understanding? Is it the lack of communication in bed that causes a marriage to break apart, or does the lack of communication start in the living room and get carried into the bedroom?

"Sex is the vehicle for relatedness," says Dr. Norman J. Levy, "and if there are problems in relatedness it shows up in the most intimate, sensitive area—sex.

"If a man has potency problems, or a woman has frigidity problems, they may bring these problems into a relationship, but that's because they've got problems in relatedness to begin with. So they bring these problems with them, and they become more intensified—and it's suddenly out in the open."

Most marriages that end up in divorce court did not get there mainly because one or the other person is an unsuitable sexual partner. People can be unsuited to each other in many ways, and if it seems that the trouble started in bed, it's only because that's where clashing personalities are at their closest.

"She Didn't Give a Damn How She Looked"

Bed, in a bad marriage, can become an unsavory battle-ground. Either person can behave vindictively, or act out feelings of anger or contempt.

One man who is happily remarried says that his ex-wife always wore a sweater to bed. "It looked awful," he said. "It was a shabby old cardigan, something that should have been thrown out years ago. I realize now it was her less obvious version of hair curlers, which really turn me off. She was saying she didn't give a damn how she looked to me. And there was another message there—she was telling me that I wasn't man enough to warm her up, no matter what I did."

One woman said that her ex-husband tried to use sex as punishment.

"We'd have a big fight, and after, when I was still furious, was when he wanted to go to bed with me. I told this to my psychiatrist, who said, 'Don't you realize that he hates you?'"

Very often, the saddest event in a bad marriage is the desperate attempt at a reconciliation—"for the children's sake," said most people, when asked why they tried so hard to hold a failing marriage together. No one said, "For my sake," or "For our sake." There was always some external factor mentioned as the reason why divorce was being desperately avoided.

"I Never Saw Her"

"I just didn't believe in divorce," said Parker E. "I believed—you're adults, you can work out your problems. I was very naïve about that. I really felt if you're two intelligent people, why can't you rekindle the flame? That's why my first wife and I went to Jamaica for four days—it was supposed to be a great reconciliation scene. And you know what? From the time we got down there to the time we left, I never saw her. I certainly never saw her in bed. But look, she had never been any hot number in bed—not for me anyway."

Parker's first wife rejected him in bed and in every other way. She kept saying that she wanted to be "free," and by that she meant free to pursue her own interests, and also to be free of Parker. She said that Parker was destroying her by his presence, because he was living evidence that she could not function in a male-female relationship. The divorce was her idea, but her decision to be free depended a great deal on Parker's generosity. She expected him to send her considerable alimony as well as child support, and even after their divorce, she still looked to Parker to cope with any problems she might have in the house that he gave her. The message, as Parker saw it, was "I don't want you, but I do want your money."

Parker's second wife, Vanessa, is the very antithesis of Parker's first wife. She's a working woman, a success in her particular field of medicine, and highly independent financially; at the same time she is very close to Parker emotionally, intellectually, and certainly sexually.

"When I met Parker, I had been around," said Vanessa. "I was twenty-eight, and in no way was I hysterical about the fact that I was still single. The idea that girls have to get married before they're twenty-one never entered my mind. Shortly before I met Parker, I had had a conversation with my cousin, who had married a man who was divorced and had a child, and I said, 'How can you do it?' and I thought I'd never go out with a man who was divorced.

"When I met Parker I knew what I wanted—absolutely knew. It was not love at first sight. I didn't love him for a couple of months, but I knew I was going to marry him. It was very, very weird—I just knew. I'd heard other people say things like that, and I'd say, 'That's ridiculous, I don't believe it.'

"We met at the craps table in Puerto Rico. My mother had just had this operation, and I'm fantastic in a crisis, but when they're over I just fall apart, and so I went to Puerto Rico, because I like to gamble. But I wasn't going to meet anybody, and I didn't want to get involved; I just went to relax. Parker had had business in Miami, and friends said, 'While you're there, why don't you go to Puerto Rico?' He wasn't interested in meeting anybody either. Anyway, we met at the craps table and he gambled a lot, and at eleven o'clock I excused myself to make a call—I was calling my mother to see how she was. And later he told me he didn't think I'd come back, but I did, and we talked, and I really talked a lot, and all of a sudden I asked him if he was married, because suddenly I thought: What if . . . ? He told me he was separated, and I thought: Fine, terrific. Then he told me he had three children, and I swallowed very hard, and I thought: This is grow-up time. This is the man, and you're going to make it—and I didn't doubt it for a minute.

"I found myself, in the beginning, highly embarrassed at how I got carried away about him—physically carried away—because I'm not that kind of a person, but he's just fabulous."

Vanessa's reaction seemed instant, chemical, and composed of the romance that many people associate with the delicious bad-good movies of the forties. But it was based on much more than that. From the very beginning, Parker and Vanessa found it easy to talk to one another, and they had much to say. Both were experienced; Parker had been married, and Vanessa had known enough other men to recognize a person who was right for her—*right* in the sense of communication on emotional and intellectual levels. They were sympathetic and sensitive to each other, and this flowed without a perceptible line of demarcation into a physical affinity.

"Nobody Was Right for Me"

A woman widowed for more than ten years described a similar scene. "After my first husband died, I went to work on Wall Street, and I met loads of men. I went out a lot, and my family was so eager to see me remarried that they were constantly introducing me to still more men. But I really never liked any of them—I mean, not for any length of time, and not deeply. I had a friend who used to make fun of me. Every time I went out with a new man she'd say, 'What was wrong with him? Too tall, too short, too thin, too fat? I know it's got to be something.' And it always was something—nothing as simple as that, of course. It was just that nobody was right for me.

"And then I met the man who became my second husband. He was married, and had two children, and I had never gone out with a married man, but there was something about Rick—I don't know if I can explain it. He was funny, but I don't mean that he told jokes, though he did that, too. His humor was so imaginative, he had a sense of fantasy, and a great zest for life—he still has. Rick enjoys things, and he made me enjoy them again. We went out a few times, and the first time he put his arm around me I wanted to burrow against his chest and go to bed with him. Nobody had made me feel that way—nobody. All the other men I had gone out with had complained I was cold.

"No, I don't feel like a home-wrecker, because Rick was terribly unhappy with his ex-wife. I don't believe a woman can take a man away from a woman if they have something going between them. We've been married eight years, and despite all the problems we've had about money, and children, and his ex-wife, it's worth it. We get angry—more at the things that come from outside to devil us than at each other—and we make up, usually in bed."

Very often a man will stay in a marriage even if the entire relationship—and therefore the sexual relationship—is bad. A woman may be quicker to insist upon a divorce. This was certainly true in the past, when there were greater moral strictures placed upon women who had extramarital affairs.

Says attorney Raoul Felder, "I've noticed over the years the difference between women and men so far as the need to get divorced. You know, for a woman everything has to be right, and if it doesn't work out, they've got to get out of it. With a man that's not so. A man has his work, and he comes home at night, and he has his food and his television set or football games, or whatever, and that's it, he's happy. He can go on for forty years that way."

According to the men who have gone on—not for forty years, but for ten and fifteen years—they have done so because they thought that was the way marriage was supposed to be. If they were unhappy sexually, they didn't analyze that unhappiness or trace it back to a basic unhappiness in their relationship; they accepted it as one of the necessary, but unpleasant, facts of life. Only after they achieved a good marriage were they made aware that another way of life was a wonderful and viable possibility.

"I never thought I was much good in bed," said Marvin P. "I mean, my wife made me feel that way—not much good. So I went looking, and I went around with a lot of other women, and some of that was okay and some of it wasn't, but none of it was really great. I never had any real confidence—not until I met the girl who became my second wife. She made me feel as though I was something really terrific, something very special—both in bed and out of it. Why did I stay married to a woman who made me feel like such a failure? I don't know. I thought that's all there was."

Many men admit, almost shamefacedly, that they are not swingers—they don't fall into bed with every available girl they meet.

"I know that most men *do*," they'll start out by saying, "but I was never like that."

The truth is that most men *don't*, but a small, slick group has forced its opinions regarding proper macho behavior on much of the male population. They've made men feel that if their sexual activity is limited to just one person they care about, something must be wrong with them.

"I Was Busy in the Office"

When Parker E. separated from his first wife, he said, "I wasn't focusing on getting remarried, or finding some other woman. Not because my analyst hadn't told me that there wasn't better stuff out there, but because some of the other guys had said, 'Take a hiatus from the world of marriage—there's all those women out there, just waiting for you,' but I wasn't interested in that kind of scene.

"I was very busy in the office, it was tax season, I had enough to keep my mind occupied, I spent a lot of time with the children. I wasn't really interested in getting involved with another woman—until I met Vanessa."

Many men describe the separation or post-divorce period as, "I felt as though I was in limbo." They knew that they were supposed to be out there, getting around, reliving bachelorhood's happiest hours, and having a good time—only they weren't. Many were lonely, felt depressed, and wanted more than a casual fling.

"I Wasn't Interested in Sleeping Around"

Dwight J. said, "What is your bench mark? What constitutes 'better'? That's what I was trying to figure out after my divorce and before my remarriage. I wasn't interested in sleeping around, I wanted something better, only I wasn't sure what that was going to be. How are you supposed to know the definition of a good marriage if you've only had one? Look, I hate to say it, but in those days I defined marriage as three-quarters misery, with an occasional pleasure. I assumed that's the way it was supposed to be."

Remarried today, Dwight says, "Now I know what's better, but I didn't have the imagination to figure it out when I was married the first time. I didn't think the way I felt was my special misery; I thought that's how everybody felt. I think if my first wife hadn't said she wanted a divorce, I might still be living with her. I was a big boy, that's how I thought of it, and I wasn't supposed to give up on a relationship."

There are some men, much older than Dwight and Parker—who are in their mid-thirties—who divorce and remarry in their fifties, sixties, and after, often in a desperate attempt to regain the sexual pleasures they feel they may have missed out on. No point in reminding them of Browning's "Grow old along with me! The best is yet to be, The last of life, for which the first was made," because they would never believe it.

"If He Has Money . . ."

Raoul Felder has stated, "It seems to me that any fifty-year-old man, if he has money, can get practically any twenty-four-year-old girl he wants."

The key words are "if he has money." This doesn't mean that a girl in her twenties can't care for a man in his fifties, but none of them seems to unless that man has money.

Felder told about one woman who made a career of marrying older men with money. "I represented a woman who was married six times. For a multiple divorcee, six is the most I've ever seen, though I didn't represent her all six times.

"She came from a coal-mining town, and she was Miss West Virginia, an extremely beautiful woman. I saw her after the sixth marriage, and she was only about thirty-eight at the time, and what happened was she got married to one guy who was a coal miner in the town she came from. She had four kids with this guy, and there was literally no food on the table, and even though she cared for him, she had to divorce him, and married a guy for the money.

"She married four other men for their money, and what happened, with all her beauty, is that the men would marry her just to conquer her, but after they married her, and the bloom was off the rose, they didn't want to get stuck with four kids. And here was this very beautiful and lovely woman, who was a little stupid, left by a progression of five men.

"But what happened is that each man was rich enough so that it paid him to get a divorce, because when the exciting sex thing wore off, there was no reason to stay with this dame. And she became wealthy in the process, but there was no ongoing wealth. She made some deals, but she had four kids, and she was very devoted to them."

"It Was a Blow to His Ego"

Comparing her first marriage to her second, Natalie J. says that though she and her first husband were married for fifteen years, by the time she asked him for a divorce, "We had had no relationship—sexual or any other kind —for years. It was a very large blow to his ego, but I was stupid for staying with him for so long. It was unfair to him. I had left once and come back, and I decided it was comfortable to say that I was married, but I had no commitment to that marriage, and I would have been much better off leaving. My present husband is so right for me, in every way. Here I am, in my late thirties, and I feel starry-eyed."

Not everyone who remarries is starry-eyed, and some women who have remarried use extramarital sex to get back at their ex-husbands. Unfortunately, very often the men who are punished are their present husbands, who have done nothing to deserve it.

"I'm Not Jealous"

"The way I look at it," said Sara H., "is that today a woman can do anything that men used to do. Nobody's going to scold her or say bad things about her. I think

I have a pretty good second marriage—I say pretty good because I don't believe anything is perfect.

"I'm still very much attracted to men who have the characteristics of my first husband—it seems to be a natural kind of pull. The men I like have this kind of intellectual, reserved nature, with a certain depth. So the second time I married a man—not necessarily deliberately, but coincidentally—who's quite the opposite. But I'm still attracted to that other kind of man."

Does Sara merely fantasize, or does she act out her fantasies in bold, living color? She admits to acting them out. No hypocrite, Sara does not say that her affairs do anything to help her second marriage or hold it together, and she admits that she could see being married for the third time if a man came along with all the qualities she admires. But the women Sara envies are the ones who never marry, and who live what Sara visualizes to be a bold, free life.

"I was really disappointed when a good friend of mine got married a couple of years ago," she said. "I thought she'd never give in—I mean never give in to that fear of being alone. I think that fear is one of the reasons I remarried—not that I can't imagine perfectly well by myself; it's just this fear.

"I learned through my second marriage that I don't need anyone—not even my present husband. I don't really need him. I want him, but I don't need him. But that took growth; when you're between your thirties and your forties is when you learn that.

"My second husband is very jealous, but I'm not jealous. I don't have a jealous nature. I like to give people a free rein. Maybe it's confidence; I don't know. Look, he comes home and sleeps with me every night, and when I need him he's there. What am I going to be jealous of? Also, I have this feeling that when a man is with me, whether it's after ten years of marriage or during a love affair, it doesn't matter. There's nothing else for him but me. There can't be—because I'm the prima."

"Aren't You Going to Ask Me About Sex?"

DAVID A.: Aren't you going to ask me about sex? I think it's one of the most important things in a marriage, and it's all tied up with compatibility, and being able to communicate. You have to be able to enjoy the same things, and understand each other. It's vital. Money is really so unimportant. If you don't have a good sex life, then why are you together? I just want to say that it's all tied in with having a good life on a lot of levels. That's what I have with my second wife. Not like with my first. My second wife didn't ask me to bring my bankbook before she'd go to bed with me, like my first wife—well, practically.

"I Would Be Willing to Forgive Him"

PAUL SILVERMAN (matrimonial lawyer): Sex doesn't always keep people together. About eight or nine years ago I represented a woman who came to me wanting a divorce because her husband was involved in an extramarital relationship to the extent that he was not at home.

And her position was, "I can't tolerate this. I would be willing to forgive him his extramarital relationship, and I'd even be willing to live with the existence of this other woman, if my husband would give me a trial sometime. If he would sort of limit himself to like Wednesday and Saturday nights with his girlfriend, and give us the other nights. I'd rather not have to tolerate it, but I think I can. But he won't do that. He's just not home at all."

So I started the case, and for a lot of reasons we didn't

call it adultery. You don't want to stigmatize a father, for
his children's sake, so we labeled his behavior as being
extremely cruel.

This man didn't know how—as a young man—to cope
with his problems, so he went in despair to his lawyer,
who was a very nice old gentleman, but who didn't com-
prehend divorce. Once you got married, you were married.

So the man's father and lawyer were working on them
to make things right, and we had a number of reconciliation kind of meetings, and they finally got the wife to say
that she would forgive him completely, and she would
forget about this episode in their lives, and she wouldn't
make him feel guilty, or talk about it, and they would live
happily ever after.

But the husband said, "I can't do this. I really don't
want to go back to my wife. Although I'm married,
although I'm the father of a child, I've come to the
realization that I've just now found out what life is all
about. I never knew that there were the erotic satisfac-
tions that I've been experiencing with my girlfriend, and
I couldn't consider abandoning her. I'll pay any price
that has to be paid, but I've got to be with my girlfriend,
and I really don't care about my wife.

"She can divorce me if she wants, she can run away
if she wants, she can kill herself if she wants, she can take
a lover if she wants. I don't care what she does. I'll give
her some money for alimony, and I'll give her some
money for child support, but my eyes have been opened
to sexual pleasures, and I have to be with this woman."

So we got the people divorced. That was something
like eight or nine years ago. This morning a woman
called and identified herself as this man's second wife.
She said, "I want a divorce from him. I'm in the process
of getting it, but my lawyer is getting cut to ribbons by

his lawyer, and I remember how you cut my husband to ribbons when he got his divorce from his first wife, and now I'd like you to do the same thing for me."

"I Used to Withdraw"

STUART I.: My first wife was very cold—always, in everything—very cold. Naturally that meant in bed, too. My second wife is warm, but she's terribly domineering. I used to withdraw—that's what I always did with my ex-wife. My second wife won't let me do that. She gets mad, she wants to fight things out. She comes after me, and we fight, and scream, and sometimes she drives me crazy! But you know, I like it. Because when we get into bed we're not lying at either side of the bed like a pair of cold mummies. No, we've yelled, we've screamed, we've fought things out, made up, and after that there's no holding back in bed.

"I Have This Drive"

WALTER R.: My second wife doesn't say no to me. I mean that. You hear all those jokes—"Not tonight, I've got a headache," or "Not tonight, I just had my hair done," only they're not really jokes, because that's what my ex-wife was like. I have this drive, this terrific sex drive, often in the middle of the night, sometimes at five, six in the morning. My wife never turns me off, never turns away. At first I was worried, I didn't think it was always so great for her—you know, like they had these scenes in the movies whenever they wanted to symbolize sex: waves pounding on the beach, a Beethoven symphony, things like that. I told her that I was worried, and she said that even if she didn't feel terrifically sexy, she always felt loving, and in that way it was good for her, too. You know what I mean? Great! Like a dummy, I told a friend of mine about it—and like a bigger dummy, he told his wife, who's a good friend of my ex's, and so everyone was talking, and my friend said that his wife said that she just couldn't be so unselfish, but she made it sound like a laugh on my wife. The hell with it—I've never been happier. And you know, about the way my wife is in bed? That's how she really is about everything. You can't separate sex from the rest of your life.

"Sex Was Something You Just Did One Way"

FERRIS Z.: My first wife made me feel that a lot of things I wanted to do in bed were dirty. Sex was something you did just one way, and that was it. Oral sex to her was dirty—disgusting. But then a lot of things I did she felt were disgusting. She'd criticize the way I ate—like if I reached for a French-fried potato with my fingers, that was a sin; things like that. She was so rigid about everything. I thought that's the way all women were, and then I met this girl, and she said that whatever two people did —with love, and if they both agreed to it—it was all right.

Let me tell you, that was a whole new world for me. I used to think that only prostitutes would have oral sex with you; now I know it's not that way at all. I'm married again, but listen, I didn't just marry that girl because she was so good for me in bed. She's like that in everything—relaxed, not uptight. What we do is our business, and she doesn't give a damn about other people. We make it together—in and out of bed.

"If I See a Man Who Appeals to Me . . ."

JEWEL M.: When I was married the first two times, my husbands really put me through hell. They did whatever they wanted to do, while I was just supposed to stay home and mind the house—and then, with my second husband, take care of our daughter. I'm married for the third time, but with some changes. It started out when I joined a consciousness-raising group for women; after that I joined NOW, and then I joined a radical feminist organization. I think you can be a feminist and still be married, only your relationship is different—you're not a rug for some man to walk over. My third husband and I share all chores around the house, and we share expenses. I'm liberated sexually, too. I work for a literary agency, and part of my job is taking people to lunch—writers and editors. And if I see a man who appeals to me, I let him know that I'd like to go to bed with him. Why not? My first two husbands did that, and I'm sure my third husband does, too. One woman I know asked me if I didn't feel that I was hurting my "sisters"—meaning the women who are married to the men I may sleep with. I know we're all supposed to be sisters in the women's movement, but I feel my sisters should learn from me. I don't think my actions would break up my third marriage, but if it should, there are plenty of other men around.

"Now I Know Why Things Were So Miserable"

ROLPH D.: I only discovered what was really wrong in my first marriage long after my ex-wife and I were divorced. My wife always ran around a lot with her girl-friends when we were married, and I didn't think anything of it. After we were divorced, she kept on—always girlfriends, never men. And then one of my sons told me, "A friend of Mommy's is moving in with us." I asked who the friend was, thinking it would be some guy, but it turned out to be a woman, Edna, a real butch type. I asked which room she was using, and my kid said, "She's sleeping where you used to sleep—with Mommy." Now my second wife and I would like to get custody of my boys; I don't think this scene is good for them, but my ex-wife clings to them—I suppose it's her last link with femininity. Anyway, now I know why things were so miserable in bed—and everyplace—with my ex, and why things are so great with my second wife. How could I have been so unaware?

X

Life Styles in Remarriage

"I was married for five years the first time, widowed for ten, and now I'm married again. I'm a lot more tolerant this time around. My second husband does things that I would have killed my first husband for doing."

Selina T., California

"I'm a lot more relaxed in my second marriage. Sure, I've changed, but as you grow older things get simpler. I don't have kids to worry about, or money, or what will the neighbors think. I'm surprised that any first marriage ever makes it—too many problems."

Werner P., Connecticut

Is there any one thing that can be said about people who remarry? Are they all blissfully happy? Do they mostly divorce and go on to try again? People are just as varied when they remarry as when they marry for the first time, and there's no stereotype among people who wed again.

What are the chances of a remarriage being a happy one? A lot depends, according to Dr. Norman J. Levy, on what he calls the "Secret agenda"—that list of hidden hopes, fears, dreams, and fantasies that people are often afraid to reveal to each other.

"Most people who get married," says Dr. Levy, "have a secret agenda—a list of all their expectations. The list contains: 'What you're going to do for me, and what I'm going to do for you if I get what I want from you.' It's very often an unspoken agenda, and it includes: 'I expect you to know my needs and fulfill them.' "

What needs? No two people have the same secret agenda, and the list can consist of such variations as:

Tell me that you love me, without my asking you to tell me that you love me.
Tell me that I'm the finest person you've ever known.
Tell me that you'll love me forever.
Tell me that you think I'm beautiful.
Tell me that you think I'm handsome.
Tell me that you think I'm brilliant.
Tell me what I need to hear, without my having to tell you what that is.

"Sometimes when people reach the second marriage," says Dr. Levy, "they realize, 'Hey, look what I'm doing,' and they're more open, more honest, and more direct."

But other times, all that openness doesn't take place until the third or possibly the fourth marriage, and some people never tell others exactly what it is they want from a relationship. Not even the most willing husband or wife can be Santa Claus or a fairy godmother without having some idea of what the other person wants. If you want those three wishes to be granted, you'd better let somebody know what they are.

The secret agenda isn't the only influence on a remarriage. On the positive side there can be a change in values, a new sensitivity toward others, a growing up, and the ability to withstand the pressures presented by family and friends. A recently added influence is the women's liberation movement, and even antifeminists can't help but be affected by the changing attitude women have toward themselves and toward men. *Husband* and *wife,* for many people, are acquiring new definitions.

"The women's liberation movement has a very big influence on the way women see themselves," says Dr. Levy, "and today not all women are willing to play the dependent part. If a woman is willing to be the pet poodle—all perked up, and gussied up, and trying to look nice on a man's arm—that's fine, but not all women are willing to do that, and that's bound to change the husband-wife relationship."

As people move out of one marriage and into another, many of them express amazement at the remarkable changes they have gone through.

"I'm a different person. . . ."

"I've learned a lot. . . ."

"I wish I had been this way during my first marriage. . . ."

That's true for many people, but not for all. Some individuals can only be comfortable with one set of cues, one kind of relationship. To fulfill their needs, they try to marry a close replica of what went before. Sometimes, as in the case of a widow or widower, that works out just fine; other times, because no two people can be truly alike, it ends in disaster.

Is there any conclusion that can be drawn from, or about, the people who remarry? Not really; their life styles are as varied as those of people who marry for the first time. It's not easy to satisfy your own needs and the needs of someone else, and there are no guarantees. Some people who remarry are happy, some are miserable. Some say, "This time is forever," others plan on trying it again, or maybe not at all. There's no one life style, no easy solution to how to live happily ever after. But if remarriage offers no single sure-fire answer, there's a great deal of hope in the thought that there are many answers—maybe enough to go around for all.

Do You Find Yourself a Very Different Person?

HILDA H. (remarried ten years): Very much so. In my first marriage I was brought up to be the sort of European wife. In that tradition I believed in the role of a wife, and I tried to fulfill that role. I had an American husband, and he didn't appreciate that particularly. Nothing I did pleased him. I decided that I never again would put myself out for a husband. I would retain my individuality at any cost, and that has nothing to do with the love I feel for my second husband.

Do You Find Any Great Difference in Your Second Marriage?

LEWIS R. (remarried seven and a half years): I think when you remarry, you really try to find a person who is right for you. There's a maturity after a first marriage —you grow up—and secondly, you know more about yourself and other people, and what you need, and how you want to live your life. You seek out or try to find someone who feels the same way. You have to mesh, you have to have that ability to communicate, which you didn't have when you were married the first time, and you were a young kid and struggling through it.

Also, you don't have to answer to anyone. You don't have to make believe. You don't have to worry about in-laws, and outlaws. It's your life now—you realize that as you get older—and you've got to make it your own life.

CHLOE R.: Also, marriage the second time isn't a completely strange thing. You've gone through it before, so you don't have to worry about all the superficial things. Lewis and I haven't got any major problems between us —there's not even a residue of problems from before. Also, I think I'm more tolerant now, and I've changed a lot, too, during and after my divorce. I became more independent, and I realized I could function as an individual. Before, during my first marriage, I thought I couldn't. At least I wasn't sure I could. I never wanted to. My ex-husband was a very domineering kind of person; you wouldn't know it to look at him—he doesn't come across that way, necessarily. He's very verbal, and I used to sit in a corner all the time. I was scared to open my mouth in company. I thought I had nothing to say. I couldn't be assertive at all. I'm a very different person. Now I never shut up, right, darling?

Do You Think You've Changed?

HARVEY J. (remarried eight years): Oh, of course. Life has changed. I was fortunate to have help from my second wife, and I was able to grow up and be able to stand on my own two feet. I've changed a lot, and I could still change some more. There's tremendous demands that we put upon ourselves.

My wife and I, we each do our own thing, but sometimes I get peeved because Marge gives too much of herself and doesn't get enough back in return. But at the same time, I understand this is Marge, and this is very good, and if there were more Marges in the world, it would be a better world. Marge and I can do things differently. I get less involved in the outside world than she does, but that's all right, too. We don't have to do everything together, or see everything in the same way.

"I Honestly Like Being Married"

THEA P. (remarried twenty years): I honestly like being married, and the thought of not being married was a very shattering thing to me. I was widowed two and a half years before I remarried.

I wanted to get married again, but I thought maybe I never would because maybe there would never be anybody who would want to marry me again. It's a strange thing, but I think you're very much looking for someone who can be somewhat like your first husband if you have been happy with him at all.

I think my second husband is a lot like my first husband—even in the weaknesses, except that my second husband is a much stronger person. My second husband likes to drink, too, but he can control it. But it's amazing —my first husband went to a prep school and then to Yale. My second husband dragged himself up with a father who didn't give a damn about him, but yet he has so many of the same qualities, the same characteristics, the same manner, as my first husband.

"We Were Ready to Kill Each Other"

GLORIA J. (remarried eighteen years): During the first five years of our marriage I never thought we would survive. We were ready to kill each other. He was difficult, I was difficult. Also, I was very dramatic. I loved living in drama, so that when we would have these dramatic confrontations I'd throw the dishes, scream, and all that other stuff. I really loved it. I know I survived on this, I adored it. But you know, we've both mellowed and matured, and today my husband is a much more compassionate person, and I'm a more understanding person, too.

Do You Think You're Different as a Wife in Your Second Marriage?

ALIX C. (remarried nine years): Yes, well, naturally. I'm older and more experienced, so I can cope. In your second marriage you're going to have the same things to cope with that you had in your first marriage, but your reactions are more mature.

In my first marriage I believed that a marriage was fifty-fifty. In my second I believe that it's ninety-ten, and it's the wife who has to give that ninety percent. And if the wife isn't willing to do this, the marriage isn't going to be very good, because men are basically very selfish creatures, and they expect women to cater to them.

Sometimes this makes me mad, but this is the male animal's way, and I'm not a women's libber at all, not at all. I like a man around the house. I want a man to love me, I want a man to take care of me and need me. And you know, I just like men. And even though I have an important job, when I go home I'm a female and a wife. When I go home I feel terribly female, and if my husband doesn't behave the way he should toward his female wife—forget about the working wife—I get very angry.

"It's a Joint Decision"

TONY A. (remarried two years): In my first marriage, I made all the decisions—everything. You don't know how tired that can make you. You're the big man, but the big man with all the troubles, all the responsibilities. My first wife, though she was bright enough, just was this helpless person. My second wife is nothing like that. I respect her, and we decide everything together. Last year my company wanted me to move to Chicago. To hell with my wife's job—they didn't even consider that. So I told them, "Look, it's got to be a joint decision, mine and my wife's. My wife is an independent girl, a modern girl, and I made many mistakes in my first marriage, and I'm not doing that again. If this is right for us as a couple, we'll go."

Well, as it turned out, I either had to move to Chicago or get another job, so I got another job, and I told my wife that she didn't even have to give me a long list of reasons why she didn't want to go to Chicago. She didn't want to go, and that was enough for me, and I said I'd never look back, or say, "Gee we should have gone," and I never have. And I wouldn't—not even if I was on a bread line someplace.

Have You Changed a Great Deal?

LUCY C. (remarried six years): I was married for seventeen years before my first husband died, and I think I'm the same person in my second marriage that I was in my first. I think I'm exactly the same as I've always been, except that I'm a Gemini, and everybody says they're two personalities, and they can change very easily and see things from both sides.

I was in business with my first husband, and I'm in business with my second, and I still work very hard, and I don't know what I would ever do if I didn't feel well enough to work.

I always say that marriage is a partnership, and partnerships in business are the most difficult things to make successful; any kind of partnership takes two people working at it awfully hard. And I don't believe in a fifty-fifty partnership—not really. I feel that I love to give one hundred percent of myself in whatever I do.

Are You a Different Wife the Second Time Around?

MARY JEAN (remarried nine years): By the time I married again, I had become a person, I had a job, a career. I had learned to manage my economics, to live alone. I remarried after having been divorced for five years, but even at the beginning of my second marriage, I was a dishcloth. I was Mrs. Adorable. I used to play the game of saying, "Honey, you'll never know that I'm working when you come home for dinner," and I'd cook these fantastic meals. I was playing out this fantasy of being the perfect wife. Now, when I come home from work exhausted, and my husband says, "What's for dinner?" I say, "I'm having cottage cheese."

When I remarried nine years ago I pretty much wanted to be in love, and I pretty much thought of marriage in terms of Sir Galahad, and the old-fashioned idea of marriage, even though it was my second marriage. Today I'm a little hostile about the whole thing, even though I know I shouldn't be, because I created a lot of what is going on.

My husband just wants to float, and I like the better life. I know that I've grown as a person, and I can stand alone through anything. I've grown through the negatives as well as the positives. I think people have to grow in their own individual ways, and if they can come together and communicate, they can make it go. If, heaven forbid, this marriage doesn't work out, I have nothing against marrying again. I'd marry again. I still feel very strongly about marriage—I don't like a different date every day, or every week. I don't like men sneaking out of my house. I didn't like it before, I never would like it again, not one bit. So marriage is, to me, the better answer.

"I'm Right Back to What I Wanted to Escape From"

HERBERT E. (remarried five years): I don't know how widespread this is, but I was greatly influenced by the knowledge that I was these three things: middle-class, Jewish, and a professional. A middle-class professional Jewish person. I earned my living going through college as a professional motorcycle racer. Now, that's not a Jewish-middle-class thing to do.

My father always wanted it made very clear that he was areligious. He referred to himself as a freethinker, which I think equates with atheism, but I'm not sure. I didn't come from a very Jewish type of background, but somehow that's how I was identified. I was a Jewish middle-class professional person, and my first wife and I did all the things that you would normally expect us to do. We owned a large, expensive house, and belonged to the temple, and did all the things our neighbors did, like putting forty dollars' worth of fertilizer on your lawn, and having a red velvet couch and green wall-to-wall carpeting. And you know, that all rankled me.

And one of the things I was escaping from by getting a divorce was that milieu. So rather deliberately I married a *shiksa*—a non-Jew. That's step number one. I was trying to do the things that would disassociate me from this middle-class Jewish existence, so the first thing that happened was that my second wife, Angela, converted to Judaism, and this had nothing to do with the fact that she married me; she just wanted to do this.

Then we rented an apartment in a predominantly Wasp community, and we moved in with all the furniture from Angela's first marriage, which I think she had bought in Woolworth's. It really was crap, and I'm selling myself on the fact that, well, at least I had escaped my middle-class Jewish life, and I'm living in this Wasp community with a Greek girl, with Woolworth furniture, and the quality of my life is really going up.

Then, as I say, Angela becomes Jewish, and when my mother comes to dinner we start getting things like *kasha varnishkes*—something even my grandmother wouldn't have thought of, and certainly not my mother, and certainly not my first wife.

And then it got to the point where Angela's Woolworth furniture started to eat at me. I couldn't stand tables made out of paper, and couches that were hard; so we went out one day, just looking around, and you know what? We ended up by buying a red velvet couch, and green carpeting for the floor.

Another thing that happened to us, we started by doing our shopping in our neighborhood supermarket, and I found out that these Wasps eat white bread and Spam. You go into this supermarket that's really big, and you find that half of it is white bread, and half of it is Spam. So I quickly came to the conclusion that I can't subsist on this, so we went to the next town, which has somewhat of a Jewish population, and we started shopping there, so we could get the food my palate was used to. Then we bought a Cadillac. Then we got very unhappy living in that Wasp community. The social life was shooting pool on Friday nights, and that would have been okay, because I really know how to do that. But then the guys—these were all my married neighbors—would all want to take off to some gin mill, where they're going to find some girls that want to get laid, and it's going to be a big Friday night, and everybody's going to get laid. That was the talk. And the four years we lived there that never happened, because we'd start shooting pool, and they'd start drinking, and within two hours they had drunk so much they had no inclination or ability to find these girls.

As the evening progressed, I shot better and better

pool, because I got to be the only one to see the ball. And I had no rapport with these people at all.

I would say, "Well, how are things?" And they would say, "All right, nothing much happened, my daughter died this week. Want to play Eight Ball?"

And I got to the point where I just couldn't relate to them at all, and we became unhappy where we were living, so we bought this house in the next town from where I had lived during my first marriage. It's got twenty-two rooms, and we're right in the middle of the middle-class professional Jewish suburban ghetto, and we have the red velvet couch, and the green wall-to-wall carpeting, and I'm on the board of the rabbinical college, but we haven't yet joined the temple. And my view of life is that I'm right back to what I wanted to escape from.

"I Don't Really Dig Pseudo Masculinity"

MAUDE O. (remarried two years): After my first husband left me, I'm the one who changed—who grew up—who learned to do for myself. My second marriage is very different from my first, and my second husband doesn't try to make me feel like the dummy I thought I was when I was married the first time.

I realize now that I was not the good, supportive wife with my first husband. You see, I talk loud, and I'm very direct, but I'm not a decisionmaker, and also, I don't really dig pseudo masculinity. I can't make a man feel like he's something that he's not. I couldn't say to my ex-husband, "Stay with me, I can't make it without you." That would have been a lie, because I didn't know how, but I knew I could make it without him.

My second husband is a lot quieter than my first, but I don't have to say to him, "We're going to do this," or "We have to do that." He tells me—he makes decisions.

If he wants to do something, or changes his mind about something, he tells me—he doesn't let things just slide along. This is what I need.

The Happy Ending?

In a way, yes, remarriages are often happier than the marriages that went before. It may seem simple, but people who remarry *want to be happy.* Didn't they want happiness the first time, or the last time around? Not always. Sometimes they married for status, for money, or because everyone in their peer group was getting married, and family and friends expected them to do the conventional thing.

There's a lot less of this business of trying to please others in a good remarriage, and much more feeling between the two people who really count—the husband and wife.

People who remarry seem to be more realistic about what they can expect from themselves and from those they marry. They understand that they're not marrying newly hatched baby chicks, but men and women with past memories, past experiences, and frequently obligations from the past. The dewy expectancies of a first marriage have disappeared, and with them, the vast disappointments when those expectancies are never completely fulfilled.

Replacing them is the ability to look at the reality of another person, another situation, and to appreciate that person more completely. There is a sense of humor in a good remarriage, an understanding and sensitivity toward the other person, and a feeling of companionship that is frequently missing from a first marriage.

"He [she] is my best friend," was something I heard frequently of partners when interviewing for this book.

That first time—or other time—around, the person wasn't supposed to be a best friend, but rather a Prince Charming, a Cinderella ("Love me, babe, and I'll dress you in diamonds"), or a Flashing Star of the Silver Screen.

Some people are accepting of each other the very first time they marry—and they're the lucky people who stay married. Most people have to learn to appreciate all the nuances that another human being is capable of, and they also must learn to recognize the real qualities that will make them happy. Not the fancy, surfacy, glossy things such as money, prestige, or golden curls, but the real things—the inner warmths and reaching out and touching that remain even if bad days come.

I have never seen such optimism as among many people who are happily remarried. It's as though *now* they know what's important to them, *now* they know what they want, and *now* they can recognize the other person who can complement them. It's that self-knowledge that gives them the strength to cope successfully with problems, and it's why a remarriage offers much more than that spurious happy ending found in fairy tales. For many people, remarriage is a wonderful happy *beginning* that can last the rest of their lives.

Index